Machine Quilting

Made Easy!

Maurine Noble

That Patchwork Place®

Credits

Editor-in-Chief . . . . Barbara Weiland
Technical Editor . . . . Ursula Reikes
Managing Editor . . . . Greg Sharp
Copy Editor . . . . Sharon Rose
Proofreaders . . . . Tina Cook
Leslie Phillips
Design Director . . . . Kay Green
Text and Cover Designer . . . . . . Dani Ritchardson
Production Assistants . . . . Shean Bemis
Claudia L'Heureux
Photographer . . . . Brent Kane
Illustrators . . . . Brian Metz
Laurel Strand
Illustration Assistant . . . . Lisa McKenney

The information in this book is presented in good faith, but no warranty is given nor results guaranteed. Since That Patchwork Place, Inc., has no control over choice of materials or procedures, the company assumes no responsibility for the use of this information.

Library of Congress Cataloging-in-Publication Data
Noble, Maurine
        Machine quilting made easy / Maurine Noble
            p.   cm. — (The joy of quilting)
        Includes bibliographical references (p.   ).
        ISBN 1-56477-074-5 :
        1. Machine quilting. I. Title. II. Series
TT835.N63 1994
746.46—dc20
94-37482
CIP

Acknowledgments

Thanks to my husband, Ed, for patiently teaching me to use the computer and helping me to solve the problems that I managed to continually produce with it. Also, for letting my passion for quilting interest him enough to enjoy accompanying me on trips to quilt shows and shops.

A special thanks to the outstanding quilters who so generously allowed me to use photos of their beautiful machine quilting in my book—Alice Allen, Caryl Bryer Fallert, Elizabeth Hendricks, Libby Lehman, Maurine Roy, and Debra Wagner. Elizabeth and Maurine are the kind of students every teacher dreams of having. Their friendship, enthusiasm, talent, and inspiration have been richly rewarding to me.

Mical Middaugh provided me with one of her lovely quilt tops to machine quilt when I didn't find time to make my own sample; thanks.

The staff at That Patchwork Place was always there to answer questions and offer encouragement. Thanks for your patience.

Machine Quilting Made Easy
©1994 by Maurine Noble
Martingale & Company
20205 144th Avenue NE
Woodinville, WA 98072-8478 USA

Printed in the United States of America
05 04 03 02   24 23 22 21 20 19

MISSION STATEMENT

We are dedicated to providing quality products and service by working together to inspire creativity and to enrich the lives we touch.

Contents

Introduction

I first became intrigued with machine quilting when I taught a basic machine embroidery class at one of the local community colleges. The class lasted eight weeks, with instructions in a different technique each week. One session was on machine quilting. All the students loved the quilting lesson and many of them returned the next week with a substantial project finished. I realized I needed to expand in this area. The time was the late 1970s, and much to my disappointment, machine quilting was not readily accepted by most quilters. I continued perfecting my skills because it was challenging to accomplish on the sewing machine what most others do by hand. I have always loved sewing machines and have upgraded my machine as technology has advanced—a total of thirteen times. Machine quilting can be done on a very simple machine, using just a straight stitch, but the computerized sewing machines available today have endless capabilities to help you do the job more easily, accurately, and with perfect control.

Harriet Hargrave is considered "The Godmother" of machine quilting. She has been teaching traditional quilting techniques on the machine since 1976, and her book *Heirloom Machine Quilting* was originally published in 1987. Barbara Johanna's *Continuous Curve Quilting* dates back to 1980, as does *The Complete Book of Machine Quilting* by Robbie and Tony Fanning.

The turning point for the general acceptance of machine quilting was in 1989 when Caryl Bryer Fallert's machine pieced and machine quilted "Corona II, Solar Eclipse" won best of show at the American Quilter's Society Show and Contest in Paducah, Kentucky. Debra Wagner's quilts have also regularly won the "machine quilted" category at AQS shows. Her impeccable machine quilting requires a second or third closeup look before one is sure it is done by machine and not by hand.

Today, an increasing number of machine-quilted quilts are being entered and are winning awards in both local and national quilt shows. Most quilters will agree that quilting is one of the most addictive pastimes they have ever pursued. The challenges of designing the quilt top, working out color and fabric choices, and choosing quilting patterns, threads, and needles are all important parts of the finished product.

Along with the popularity of home sergers came the introduction of a wide variety of beautiful decorative threads. Most of these threads can also be used on the sewing machine to enhance the effect of quilting. Machine quilting has its own unique charm and character. I believe that if you machine quilt a quilt, you may as well make it look like machine quilting. It is not always necessary to try to imitate hand quilting. Books and magazine articles have been my inspiration and learning source. Some of my favorites are listed on page 63.

How to Use This Book

This book is designed to guide you through the basics of machine quilting. Exercises are provided along the way so that you can try the various techniques. It is important to work through all of the exercises to fully understand the possibilities, to learn how your machine responds to various threads, and to determine how to set the tension for a balanced stitch. Give yourself time to experiment, to play, and then to practice. By doing all of the exercises and making the samples, you will learn the basics and have samples to refer to later when choosing among the various techniques.

Don't expect to jump right in and quilt your first top without practicing. You'll only become frustrated. It's much better to experiment with the stitch length and tension on a practice piece than on your quilt top. Once you've learned the basics, you will soon be able to see that the design possibilities of and applications for machine quilting are endless.

For each of the sixteen exercises, you will need a 14" square of muslin for the top, a 14" square of batting, and a 14" square of fabric for the back. You may want to cut several of these beforehand so that you have them ready. Layer them together to make a quilt sandwich and use a few safety pins to baste the layers together. In some exercises you will need to draw on the muslin before layering and pinning.

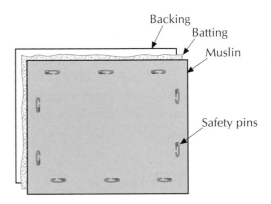

Supplies

Threads

Choosing thread is one of the most important decisions you will make when preparing to machine quilt. Thread may be strictly utilitarian or it may be an important part of the quilt's decorative design.

In hand quilting, most of the quilting thread is buried between the layers of the quilt, with only a bit visible on the quilt top and bottom. When a quilt is machine quilted, a continuous line of thread is visible on the top and back surfaces of the quilt. If regular-weight sewing thread or hand quilting thread is used, the surface may look too "thready" for traditional-looking quilting, but this may be just what you want for a more decorative look.

For traditional machine quilting, I prefer to use a lightweight cotton thread, because it has the same fiber content as the fabric and blends well with the quilt. Polyester thread is stronger than the cotton fabric in the quilt, and may in time cause the fabric to weaken and wear around the quilting line. If the quilt calls for dense quilting with lots of background stitching, like the Feathered Star quilt on page 32, you will want to choose the lightest-weight thread you can find. If you are only stitching a diagonal line every 2" to 4", you should use a stronger thread so the stitching line will not weaken and break when the quilt is used.

Threads are numbered so the lightest weight thread has the highest number; just the opposite from the way needles are sized. The numbers 60/2 on a spool of thread mean that it is two twisted strands of a 60-weight thread. Not all spools give you this information. To determine the weight of an unmarked spool, compare it, by feel and sight, to a thread that has a known weight. When the ply is not indicated in the number on the spool, it is most likely a two-ply thread. It is important to use threads of similar weight when using two different kinds of thread, for example a 60/2 Mettler in the bobbin and invisible thread on the top spool. The tension will naturally balance with similar or equally weighted threads.

Before beginning any project, it is always a good idea to make a sample quilt sandwich out of the same backing, batting, and top fabrics you plan to use in the quilt. This gives you an opportunity to try marking tools, threads, needles, and quilting patterns. It also gives you a chance to practice before you begin on the real thing.

Lightweight Threads—
Threaded through the Needle

The threads listed in Table 1 on page 57 work well for traditional machine quilting. I have listed them by weight, beginning with the lightest weight, and have included the yardage on each spool. Many other brands are manufactured; these are just the most readily available.

Bobbin Threads

The bobbin threads listed in Table 1 were originally intended for use in the bobbin for lingerie and machine embroidery. They are fine in weight and very strong. I often use bobbin threads when machine quilting because they do a better job of controlling top threads that are difficult to use, like some of the metallics. These bobbin threads can also be used in the needle for fine, almost invisible stitching. When using heavier decorative threads in the bobbin, these threads may work on the top. Try various combinations of threads on the top and in the bobbin to determine which threads are compatible.

Decorative Threads—
Threaded through the Needle

If you want the thread to be very visible and give a decorative look to the quilting, you will want to use a heavier and/or decorative thread. These threads give varying effects and highlights to your quilt top. The threads listed in Table 2 on pages 58–59 are some of my favorites for decorative machine quilting.

Decorative Threads—
Used in the Bobbin or Couched

Another category of thread appropriate for decorative machine quilting or machine couching is the heavier threads that are designed to be used on the loopers of a serger. Most cannot, however, fit through the eye of a machine needle. For machine quilting, wind these threads on the bobbin and place your quilt top side down. Use a strong top thread with this technique, such as Mettler Silk Finish, Mettler Metrosene Plus, or J. & P. Coats Plus® Extra Fine Dual Duty, or one of the bobbin threads listed in Table 1.

Heavy thread can also be couched in single or multiple strands onto the top surface of the quilt by machine. See Table 3 on page 60 for a list of threads suitable for use in the bobbin or for couching.

Needles

Sewing machine needles are numbered 70/10, 80/12, 90/14, and so on. The numbers indicate the size of the needle. A fine needle has a lower number, and a larger needle has a higher number. The first number (90) is from the European numbering system; the second number (14) is from the American system. Needle sizes 70/10 and 80/12 are normal for stitching seams as well as for machine quilting with lightweight cotton or invisible thread. When quilting with metallic and other decorative threads, it is necessary to use a larger-sized specialized needle.

It is helpful to try a variety of machine needles to determine which one works best on your quilt sample. If the thread shreds, try using a needle with a larger eye. Begin with the finest needle in the group indicated for the type of thread you are using. (See Tables 1 and 2 on pages 57–59 for needle suggestions.) If the thread begins to shred or break, change to the next larger size. Continue this process until you find the right combination. Expect to change your needle often. I usually try two, sometimes three needles before I find the perfect one. Some useful sewing machine needles are listed in Table 4 on page 61. All are made by Schmetz except the metafil needle by Lammertz.

> *Tip:* Always insert a new needle when beginning a project and clean and oil your machine regularly.

Walking Foot or Even-Feed Foot

A walking/even-feed foot (or dual-feed arm) prevents tucks from forming in the quilt top and backing as you machine quilt. A walking foot has a movable arm that rests above, or a movable forked arm that fits around the needle screw on the right side of the needle bar of your machine. As the needle bar moves up and down, it lifts the center section of the walking foot, then drops it down to grab the fabric and pull it in a backward motion with the feed dogs. This releases the presser foot pressure on the quilt sandwich to keep the foot from pushing the top layer of your quilt forward as you stitch.

The part of the foot which comes in contact with the fabric (the bottom side of the center section) may be smooth or it may have "teeth" or a rubberized surface. The "teeth" or rubberized surface help to grab the fabric and pull it along. This is especially helpful for quilts with heavier battings. This movable section of the walking foot should line up perfectly with the feed dogs on your machine, as the foot and feed dogs work together to move the quilt sandwich along as you stitch. The size of the screw head or the length of the presser foot screw may prevent a walking foot from fitting correctly. In this case, purchase a shorter-length screw with a smaller head or a longer screw with a larger head for your machine.

Some sewing-machine manufacturers make a walking foot designed especially for their machines. If one is available for your make, this is the foot to purchase. If you have a sewing machine with a dual-feed arm, you don't need a walking foot.

Other machines can usually be fitted with a generic walking foot. First you must determine if your machine has a low, high, or slant-needle shank. Refer to your instruction book to determine this. Be aware that some walking feet are more effective than others, so be sure you can exchange or return a foot before you buy it.

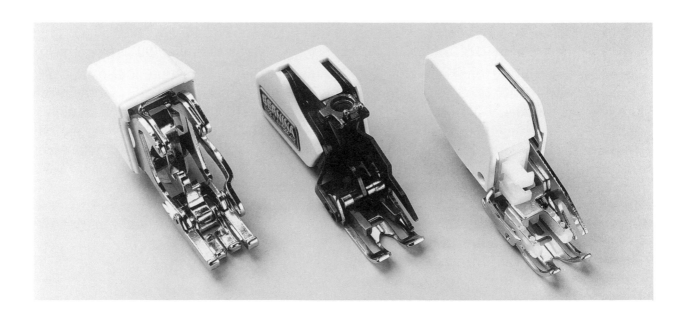

Darning Foot

A darning foot is required for freehand quilting. Most sewing machines come equipped with a darning foot. The up-and-down movement of the needle bar raises and lowers the foot, holding the quilt sandwich firmly against the base of the machine as the needle and bobbin threads lock to form a stitch, then releases the fabric, so you can move the quilt between stitches. Without a darning foot, the quilt would have to be held tautly in a hoop; otherwise, the stitch tension would be uneven and could cause skipped stitches.

It is important to have as much visibility as possible when freehand quilting. Darning feet are often closed circles; however, some manufacturers do make darning feet that are open in front. If an open foot is not available for your machine, you can have the front part of your darning foot cut out to improve visibility. See your sewing machine dealer to do this. Low-shank, clear plastic darning feet are also available and can be substituted for the metal feet that come with some machines.

Quilting Techniques

Straight-Line Quilting

Straight-line quilting (unlike freehand quilting) is done with the feed dogs up, or engaged. This is why you need the walking foot—to counteract the constant tugging on the bottom quilt layer. Since the feed dogs are engaged, the machine is pulling the fabric through in one direction. This technique therefore works best for designs with long, continuous, fairly straight quilting lines. Stitching in-the-ditch, simple outline quilting, and channel or grid quilting are good examples. You can turn wide curves, and you can pivot just as you do in regular sewing, but you can't turn tight curves.

When you use a walking foot, the machine not only controls the direction, it also controls the stitch length. It is important to set the machine for a longer stitch length than you would use to sew a seam. To start and end a line of quilting, adjust the machine to a very short stitch length, sew 8 to 10 stitches, then snip off the thread ends close to the quilt surface. Unlike other methods, this one ties off the quilting line effectively without making an unsightly knot or leaving thread ends to be concealed.

Exercise 1

Determining the Stitch Length

Stitch length settings vary with different brands of sewing machines. Here is a way to test the stitch length on your machine.

☐ 1. Using a fine-point marker, draw 2 sets of lines on a 14" square of muslin, as shown. Draw the first set of lines ¼" apart and the second set of lines 1" apart.

☐ 2. Layer the marked muslin square with batting and backing; secure with safety pins.

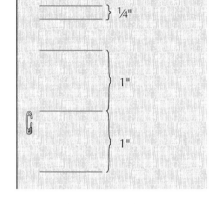

☐ 3. Attach the walking foot to your sewing machine and set the stitch length at .5mm or to the smallest setting at which the fabric still advances. Stitch between the first lines (¼") and count the stitches. Adjust the stitch length until you get 14 to 16 stitches within the ¼" space. You will use these short stitches to "tie off" at the beginning and end of a line of quilting. When you tie off, you will only make 8 to 10 short stitches, so the distance covered will be less than ¼". Note the setting on your machine so you can repeat the tie-off again and again.

☐ 4. Repeat the same procedure with the second set of lines, but begin with a stitch length of 2.50mm, 2.75mm, or 3mm or 10 to 11 stitches per inch. Stitch within the 1" spaces until you can consistently get 10 to 11 stitches per inch.

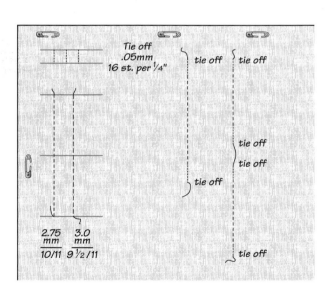

☐ 5. Stitch a few practice lines: begin with a tie-off, quilt a distance, and end with a tie-off. Do this until you can change the stitch length on your machine easily and smoothly. You can also learn to increase and decrease the stitch length while you are stitching rather than stopping the machine, changing the stitch length, then starting again.

> *Tip:* If your sewing machine allows you to preprogram stitch lengths and will recall that information, take advantage of this time-and-motion-saving feature. I set my straight stitch length on 2.75mm for quilting and program my zigzag stitch to 0 stitch width and .5mm stitch length to tie off. That way, I only need to go back and forth between the two programmed stitch settings as I tie off, stitch, and tie off. The machine remembers the stitch length changes for me.

When straight stitching with a walking foot, you may have a problem with the foot "hanging up," or making smaller stitches when sewing over a heavy lump of seam allowances. When this happens, stop the machine with the needle in the fabric, lift the presser foot up, drop it back down, and continue stitching. The extra thickness of fabric in the seam allowances may prevent the foot from moving properly, but as soon as the fabric is released it will move along as it should.

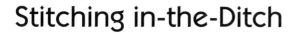

Exercise 2

Stitching in-the-Ditch

One of the easiest and most popular methods of machine quilting is stitching in-the-ditch. The quilting simply follows the seams in or between blocks and there are no lines to mark. Each seam has a low and a high side, created by the seam allowances being pressed to one side. The low side, or "ditch," is the side without seam allowances. Learning to stitch "in-the-ditch" takes some practice.

☐ **1.** Fold a 14" square of muslin in quarters and sew 3 seams on the back side of the fabric, ¼" away from each fold. Press the seams to one side. It is very important to press seams completely flat so that there is no fold or overlap on the top side of the ditch.

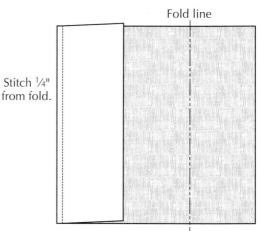

Fold line

Stitch ¼" from fold.

☐ **2.** Layer the seamed square of muslin with batting and backing fabric; secure with safety pins.

☐ **3.** Stitch as close as you can on the low side of the seam line. It is a challenge to keep from riding onto the high side. This can best be avoided by slowing down the machine speed and carefully watching and guiding the quilt. Use your hands to gently spread the seams without distorting them while you stitch.

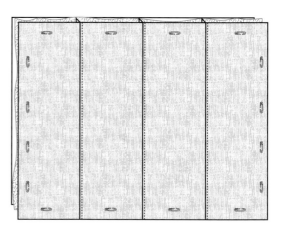

Tip: When stitching in-the-ditch, you will inevitably run across seams that have been pressed in opposite directions on two sides of an intersecting seam. This means that the low side of the seam line will change sides. If the intersecting seams do not match, take one or two stitches to the left or right, so that you are always stitching on the low side of the seam.

Many patterns can be quilted by machine with a walking foot. A few of the more traditional ones are included in Exercise 3.

Exercise 3

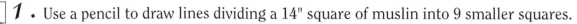

Background Quilting Sampler

☐ **1.** Use a pencil to draw lines dividing a 14" square of muslin into 9 smaller squares.

☐ **2.** Layer the marked muslin square with batting and backing fabric; secure with safety pins.

☐ **3.** Make a sampler by stitching a different pattern in each square. You can draw lines to follow or use a quilting guide attachment on your walking foot if you have one. Remember to tie off at the beginning and end of each row of stitching. Start in the center square and remove pins when they get in your way.

You may find that you like stitching some patterns more than others. Practice the ones that you like on small practice quilt sandwiches before attempting to machine quilt a whole quilt top.

Freehand Quilting

Freehand quilting is a very different experience from straight-line quilting. In this technique you control the direction of the stitches and the length of the stitches by moving the quilt forward and back and sideways under the needle. With a little practice it is possible to quilt any pattern on the machine that was once deemed only possible by hand.

Both contemporary and traditional quilters are using this technique extensively to enhance the surfaces of their quilts. Debra Wagner's quilt (page 32) is an excellent example of traditional quilting done freehand, and Caryl Bryer Fallert's and Libby Lehman's quilts (pages 29 and 30) are wonderful examples of the range of possibilities for freehand quilting with a contemporary feel.

If you have never used a darning foot or worked freehand on your machine, you have an exciting experience ahead of you.

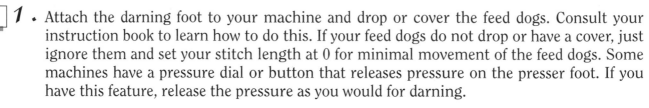

Exercise 4

Freehand Quilting

1. Attach the darning foot to your machine and drop or cover the feed dogs. Consult your instruction book to learn how to do this. If your feed dogs do not drop or have a cover, just ignore them and set your stitch length at 0 for minimal movement of the feed dogs. Some machines have a pressure dial or button that releases pressure on the presser foot. If you have this feature, release the pressure as you would for darning.

   When the feed dogs are dropped or covered and the presser foot is lowered, there should be room between the bottom of the darning foot and the bed of the machine to move the fabric freely.

2. Prepare a 14" quilt sandwich (page 5). Mark 12, 3, 6, and 9 o'clock positions on your practice quilt sandwich, just like the face of a clock. See illustration below.

3. Place the fabric with the 6 o'clock mark closest to your lap. Starting in the middle of the square, bring the bobbin thread to the top of the quilt sandwich so it doesn't tangle or jam on the back side. If your machine has a single stitch feature, take one stitch, holding the top thread, and pull the bobbin thread through the fabric to the top.

   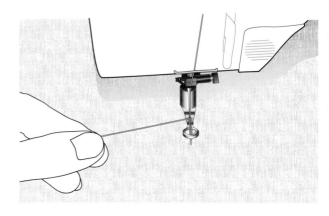

   If your machine does not have this feature, hold the top thread while turning the hand wheel toward you through one complete rotation. When the sewing machine take-up lever is in its highest position, pull the bobbin thread to the top.

4. Hold the top and bobbin threads for the first few stitches to prevent tangling. Run the machine as you move the fabric slowly to make 8 to 10 small stitches within a ⅛" distance. You are tying off, just as you did with the walking foot, but now it is no longer the machine, but you who control the stitch length. It doesn't matter where the stitch length is set on your machine, because the feed dogs are dropped or covered and cannot move the quilt. After tying off, cut off the thread tails.

5. Now you are ready to play! Begin stitching while moving the fabric sideways, back and forth, and in a circular motion, always keeping the 6 o'clock side of the fabric parallel to the front edge of the machine.

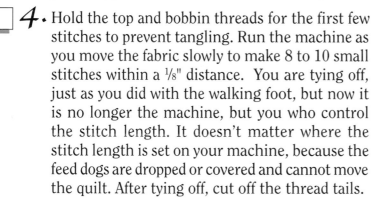

12

9

3

6

More About Freehand Quilting

Remember that when you work on an actual quilt, you cannot turn the quilt to stitch around a block or in a circular motion, because half of the quilt will be rolled into the opening in the body of the machine.

Think of the sewing machine needle as a pencil. You can draw circles with the needle without turning the fabric in a circular motion, just as you can draw a circle on a piece of paper by keeping the pencil (needle) stationary while moving the paper (quilt).

While you practice drawing with your needle, you must also be aware of the speed of the machine in relation to the speed with which you move the fabric. You may want to set the speed of the machine motor to slow or half speed if you have this option.

Running your machine too slowly will cause uneven, jerky-looking stitches. If you move the fabric very fast while running the machine slowly, you will have long stitches. If you move the fabric very slowly while running the machine at a fast speed, you will have tiny stitches. Your goal is to develop a rhythm so your stitches are relatively even in length and you can make smooth curves and lines as you draw with your needle. When you're first learning, push yourself to run your machine faster than is comfortable, and you will develop control sooner. I set my machine on two-thirds speed and "floor" the foot control. This is perfect for me, and I don't have to think about controlling the speed, just moving the fabric.

Sewing in your stocking feet gives you a better feel for the foot control and the speed of the machine. The newer sewing machines have advanced electronics in the foot controls that enable you to stitch one stitch or a half stitch at a time and to speed up or slow down with a gentle application or release of foot pressure.

You may feel tense when you first begin to work freehand with your machine. Don't panic. This is a completely different way of using your sewing machine. Your hands and brain need to get used to moving the fabric. The machine has always done this for you when you have sewn "normally." You will have an overwhelming feeling of freedom as you become more and more adept at controlling the motion and stitch length. Stitch control will develop with practice. It will take time, so don't give up.

If you find it difficult to move the quilt on the bed of your machine, try using rubber fingertips (file fingers) on one or several fingers of each hand, or try surgical gloves or lightweight cotton gloves. Any of these items gives you leverage to help move the quilt. To control the movement of the quilt as I am freehand quilting, I place my left hand flat against the quilt and bed of the machine, to the left and in front of the needle. I use my right hand to grab a handful of the quilt behind the needle.

Your sewing machine has now become a creative tool. You have opened the door to a whole new world of freehand technique possibilities. When you have drawn with your needle for a while and feel some confidence in what you are doing, it is time to work with a printed fabric that has definite lines in the design.

Tip: Don't forget to breathe, let yourself go, and have fun!

$\mathcal{E}xercise\ 5$

Following a Printed Line

A landscape print is a good choice for practicing this technique.

☐ *1.* Cut a 14" square from a printed fabric; layer with batting and backing and secure with safety pins.

☐ *2.* This is a good opportunity to experiment with invisible nylon thread. This thread is available in clear, for light-colored fabrics, and in smoke, for darker-colored fabrics. Nylon thread can be used on the top spool or bobbin of a machine, or in both places at once. It is very fine, stretchy, and difficult to see. Once you have conquered threading the needle and can find the thread, you are on your way to success. Because it is stretchy, wind it on the bobbin at a slower speed than usual. The needle thread tension will need to be loosened (lowered) at least one number. Remember to tie off the thread each time you start and stop a line of quilting. You do not have to cut the threads or pull the bobbin thread to the top side when moving from one place to another on the quilt. Just lift the presser foot to release the thread tension, move on to the next area you want to stitch, and drop the presser foot. After tying off the thread, snip the loose threads if they are in your way.

If the nylon thread starts to tangle, pull tightly, or get caught on the spool pin, remove the thread from the machine's spool pin and set it on a thread stand or in a coffee mug behind the right side of the machine. The thread is cross-wound on the spool and pulls up off the spool more easily than sideways.

☐ *3.* Start in the center of the piece and follow the design lines in the print. You can quilt around some or all of the shapes in the print. Keep the fabric oriented in the same position, moving the fabric sideways, forward, and backward.

Don't worry about stitches that wander off the printed lines. This isn't an heirloom quilt you are working on—just a practice piece. Allow yourself play and practice time to become comfortable with this technique. You may want to practice by quilting two or three "cheater" panels or preprinted quilt pieces. This gives you the freedom to play and develop skills without being intimidated by or nervous about working on a quilt top that is precious to you. Preprinted baby or lap quilts make great gifts, especially for non-quilters.

Tip: Be good to yourself by using printed fabric for the quilt backing while you are perfecting your machine quilting skills. Mistakes and uneven stitches are difficult to see on a print, but are very visible on a solid fabric.

Exercise 6

Continuous Pattern Quilting

Now that you are feeling much more comfortable with freehand quilting, it is time to try a more challenging project.

1. Trace the leaf pattern below in the center of a 14" x 14" square of muslin by making a dotted line pattern with a washable marker.

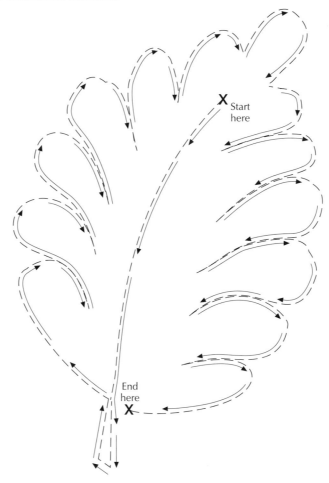

X Start here

End here X

2. Layer the muslin with batting and backing; secure with safety pins.

3. Quilt the continuous pattern on the dotted line, following the direction of the arrows. Be sure to avoid turning the fabric; move sideways, backward, and forward only. You will be double stitching a small portion of each lobe of the leaf pattern. It may be difficult at first to stitch exactly on the marked line, but be patient with yourself. Draw another pattern on another piece of muslin and try again. Practice is a wonderful teacher.

The practice piece you just made is a perfect central motif to highlight with background quilting or grid quilting. Always quilt the motif or outline the appliqué pattern before you begin the background stitching.

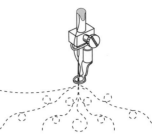

Exercise 7

Learning to Stipple

Stippling is one of the easiest and most effective of the background patterns. First we'll practice stippling, then move on to filling in the background of our central motif. Play with stippling until you feel in control. Everyone can learn to stipple well.

1. Change the thread in your machine to a lightweight cotton. DMC 50™ or Mettler embroidery thread are good choices. Choose a contrasting thread if you want to really see your stitches. Fill the bobbin with the same thread. Adjust your top tension to a normal setting.

2. Prepare a 14" quilt sandwich (page 5.)

3. Start stitching in the center of the quilt sandwich, moving the fabric back and forth and right and left. Traditional stippling uses a continuous motion to form wiggly shapes that look like jigsaw puzzle pieces. The stitching lines should not cross or look too uniform.

Stippling can be done in any scale you desire. Try making the lines closer together, then farther apart. A tiny stippling pattern will flatten out and fill in the background. A larger stippling pattern can be used as an allover quilting pattern. At first it may be difficult to make smooth curves; this will come with practice.

4. Practice stippling in various sizes until you feel comfortable moving the fabric around and your stitches are relatively even. Then use the piece made in Exercise 6 and fill in the background with stippling. Try stippling in different scales to see the effects they have.

The white-on-white sampler below illustrates 4 different background treatments surrounding a central motif. These were done freehand without marking. Try some of your own on another quilt sandwich.

Exercise 8

Freehand Quilting Sampler

Make a sampler of different freehand quilting patterns. Copy the ones shown, alter them, or design your own.

☐ **1.** Use a pencil to draw lines dividing a 14" square of muslin into 9 smaller squares.

☐ **2.** Layer the marked muslin square with batting and backing fabric; secure with safety pins.

☐ **3.** Quilt a different pattern in each square. Start in the center square and remove pins when they get in your way.

Exercise 9

Quilting a Feather Wreath

This exercise will show you how to quilt a traditional feather wreath two different ways. Dissecting patterns and figuring out different ways they can be stitched is the best way to plan for machine quilting and will increase your options enormously.

☐ *1*. For the first feather wreath, trace the design below onto a 14" square of muslin so that the feathers do not quite touch. This is the usual way wreaths are drawn for machine quilting. Layer the muslin, batting, and backing; secure with safety pins.

☐ *2*. Stitch along the drawn lines. Notice that the lines do not touch and the feathers are separated.

3. For the second feather wreath, trace the design below onto a 14" square of muslin so that the feathers are very tight against each other. Layer the muslin, batting, and backing; secure with safety pins.

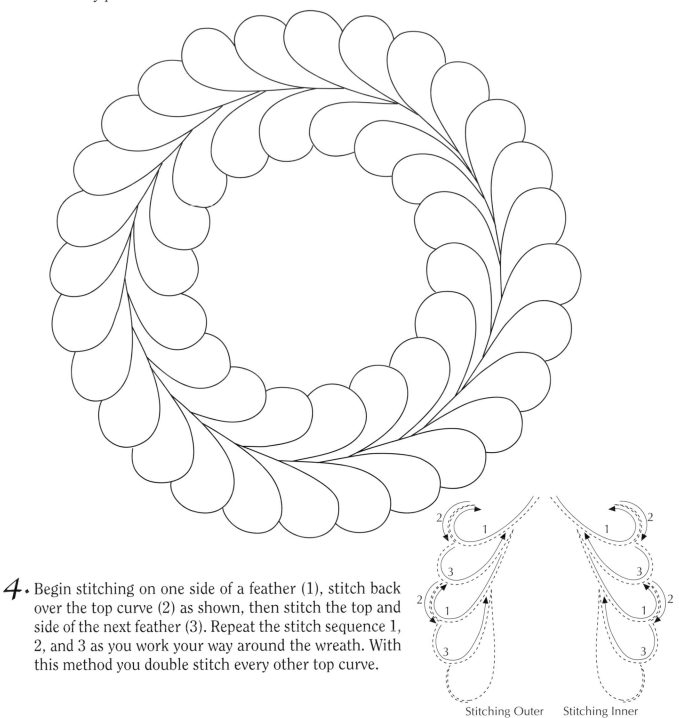

Stitching Outer Feathers   Stitching Inner Feathers

4. Begin stitching on one side of a feather (1), stitch back over the top curve (2) as shown, then stitch the top and side of the next feather (3). Repeat the stitch sequence 1, 2, and 3 as you work your way around the wreath. With this method you double stitch every other top curve.

There are no wrong ways to machine quilt, but there are easier ways. You are the judge of your own work. Most of us are very hard on ourselves and are our own worst critics. Perfection comes with practice.

Quilting with Decorative Threads

Threads with a variety of sheens and textures can add a special look to your quilting. Decorative threads are composed of rayon, mylar, wool, silk, acrylic, polyester, and cotton, in different weights and thicknesses, and can be used on a sewing machine. You can use the lightweight threads in the needle, but you must feed heavyweight threads through the bobbin or couch them onto the surface.

Be sure you are confident with your machine and your skill level before you use these threads, which will dominate the quilt surface.

Hints for Using Lightweight Decorative Threads in the Needle

- Choose the correct needle for the thread you are using and fill the bobbin with a similar-weight thread.

- Stitch with the machine at half speed, or slower than usual.

- Choose a simple, long stitch to show off the thread.

- Adjust the top tension if necessary.

- Always make a sample first to determine the best stitch, stitch length and width, tension, and needle for the thread and materials you are using.

Exercise 10

Determining Tension Settings
for Lightweight Decorative Threads

☐ **1.** Mark a 14" square of muslin with 10 horizontal lines and label them 1–9 as shown, or use numbers that correspond with the thread tension numbers on your machine.

☐ **2.** Layer the marked muslin with batting and backing; secure with safety pins.

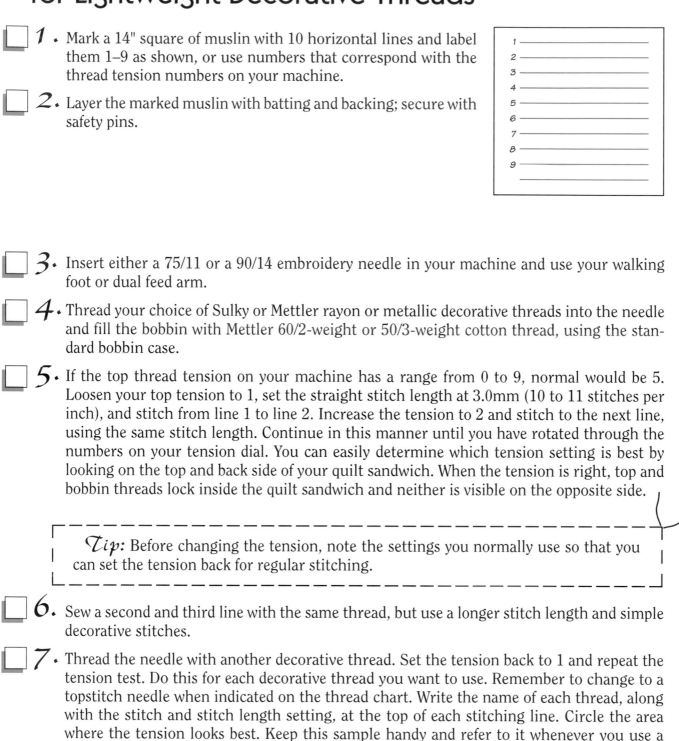

☐ **3.** Insert either a 75/11 or a 90/14 embroidery needle in your machine and use your walking foot or dual feed arm.

☐ **4.** Thread your choice of Sulky or Mettler rayon or metallic decorative threads into the needle and fill the bobbin with Mettler 60/2-weight or 50/3-weight cotton thread, using the standard bobbin case.

☐ **5.** If the top thread tension on your machine has a range from 0 to 9, normal would be 5. Loosen your top tension to 1, set the straight stitch length at 3.0mm (10 to 11 stitches per inch), and stitch from line 1 to line 2. Increase the tension to 2 and stitch to the next line, using the same stitch length. Continue in this manner until you have rotated through the numbers on your tension dial. You can easily determine which tension setting is best by looking on the top and back side of your quilt sandwich. When the tension is right, top and bobbin threads lock inside the quilt sandwich and neither is visible on the opposite side.

> *Tip:* Before changing the tension, note the settings you normally use so that you can set the tension back for regular stitching.

☐ **6.** Sew a second and third line with the same thread, but use a longer stitch length and simple decorative stitches.

☐ **7.** Thread the needle with another decorative thread. Set the tension back to 1 and repeat the tension test. Do this for each decorative thread you want to use. Remember to change to a topstitch needle when indicated on the thread chart. Write the name of each thread, along with the stitch and stitch length setting, at the top of each stitching line. Circle the area where the tension looks best. Keep this sample handy and refer to it whenever you use a lightweight decorative thread in your quilt.

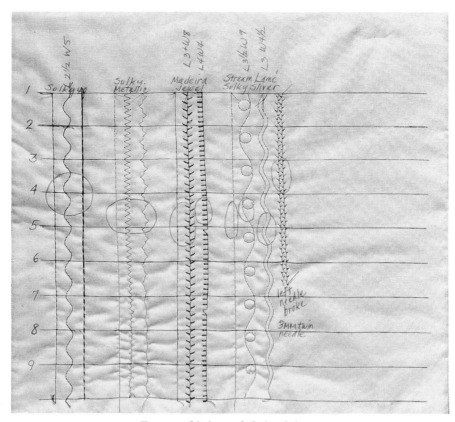

Front Side of Stitching

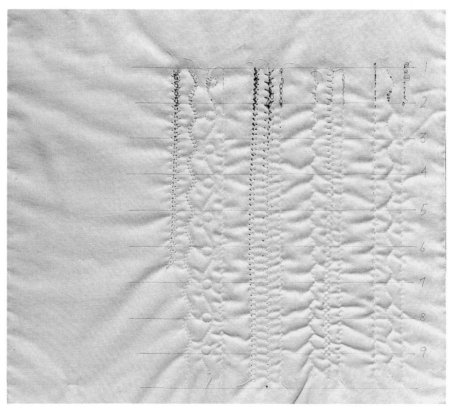

Wrong Side of Stitching

Lightweight Threads

Some of the lightweight decorative threads, especially the rayons, allow you to thread two strands of thread through the eye of the needle. This gives a heavier, more dominant quilting line. The two threads may be the same color or a combination of plain and variegated colors. Another way to achieve a heavier line with light-weight thread is to use a straight stretch stitch. This stitch moves forward and backward while you stitch, forming a triple stitch (three threads on the surface). Use the long stitch feature, if your machine has one, to get a double-length triple stitch, which resembles a saddle stitch. This is especially effective with variegated rayon thread.

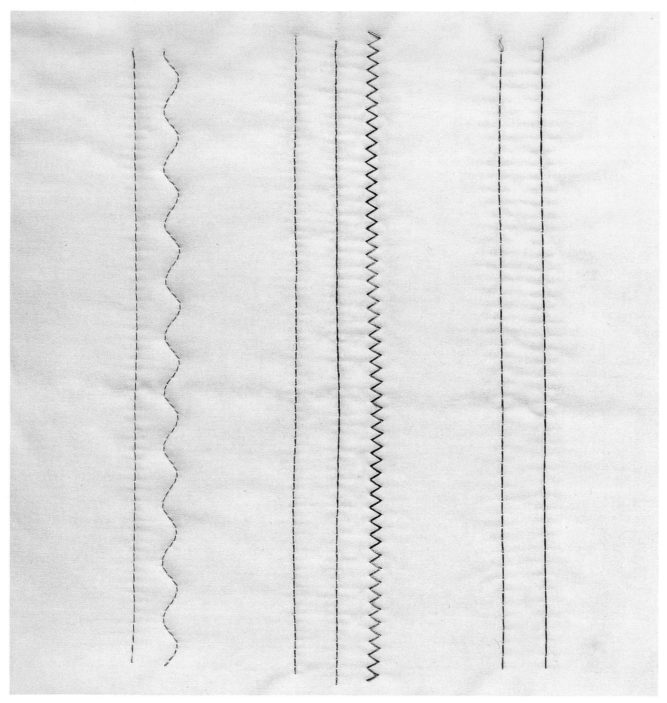

2 strands through needle,
straight stitch, and
running stitch

1 strand thread,
triple stitch, straight,
and zigzag

1 strand thread,
long, triple stitch

Decorative Threads in the Bobbin

If a heavier thread won't go through the needle, it is time to try it in the bobbin. A separate or adjustable bobbin case is necessary for this technique, because you will need to adjust the tension on the bobbin case. Keep one bobbin case set at normal tension for your regular stitching and purchase a second bobbin case to use when you want to adjust bobbin tensions. To help you keep track of them, some sewing machine manufacturers make a bobbin case with a black latch to differentiate it from the normal one. You can also paint the latch on a second bobbin case with colored nail polish.

To adjust the tension, use a small screwdriver. Turn the screw to the left (counter-clockwise) to loosen, and to the right (clockwise) to tighten.

Remember this by saying to yourself "lefty loosey, righty tighty." It is possible to loosen the screw so much that it falls out. If this happens, watch it carefully, as it is small and easy to lose.

Use the bobbin winder on your sewing machine to fill the bobbin. If the thread is too heavy to run smoothly through the thread winding guide, hold the spool in your lap and hand guide the thread as the bobbin winds. Do not overfill the bobbin, as it must fit easily into the bobbin case. Place the filled bobbin in the extra bobbin case the usual way, pulling the thread into the tension disk. Loosen the tension screw by turning it to the left until the thread pulls through the bobbin tension disk easily. To test the tension, hold the thread with one hand and let the bobbin and case dangle. The bobbin case should drop slightly when you jerk the thread. If not, adjust the tension again.

Note: If you have a bobbin case that is not removable, contact your dealer to find out how to adjust the bobbin tension.

Hints for Using Decorative Threads in the Bobbin

- Wind the bobbin slower than usual because the threads are delicate. Do not overfill the bobbin.

- Stitch with the back side of the quilt facing you and the top side of the quilt facing the feed dogs.

- Use a sharp needle and a strong thread in the top. A fine, strong bobbin thread or polyester sewing thread are good choices for heavy top embellishment. See Table 1 on page 57 for various bobbin threads.

- Adjust the top tension to make the decorative bobbin thread look as if it is stitched into the quilt, not just lying on the surface.

- Machine stitch at a slow speed.

- Use a simple, long stitch to make the thread more visible.

- Thread the loose beginning and ending threads into a hand needle and weave them into the batting of the quilt.

Gallery of Quilts

The quilts in the gallery have been selected to provide inspiration only. There are no specific patterns or instructions provided for the techniques of other quilters.

Caryl Bryer Fallert continually introduces new concepts as she creates unique contemporary quilts from her own hand-dyed fabrics. Her whole-cloth quilt is an exceptional example of using unmarked freehand machine quilting as an important design element.

Libby Lehman gives us a whole new look at quilting with decorative threads. Her quilts literally shine with glitz and color.

Debra Wagner's traditional machine quilting techniques are flawless—and almost unbelievable.

Alice Allen shows us that we can mix quilting patterns to make an attractive garment while practicing new techniques. She is a master of precision machine-decorative stitching.

Elizabeth Hendricks and Maurine Roy are students of mine who amaze me with their talent and ability to produce beautiful and innovative quilts by the dozens.

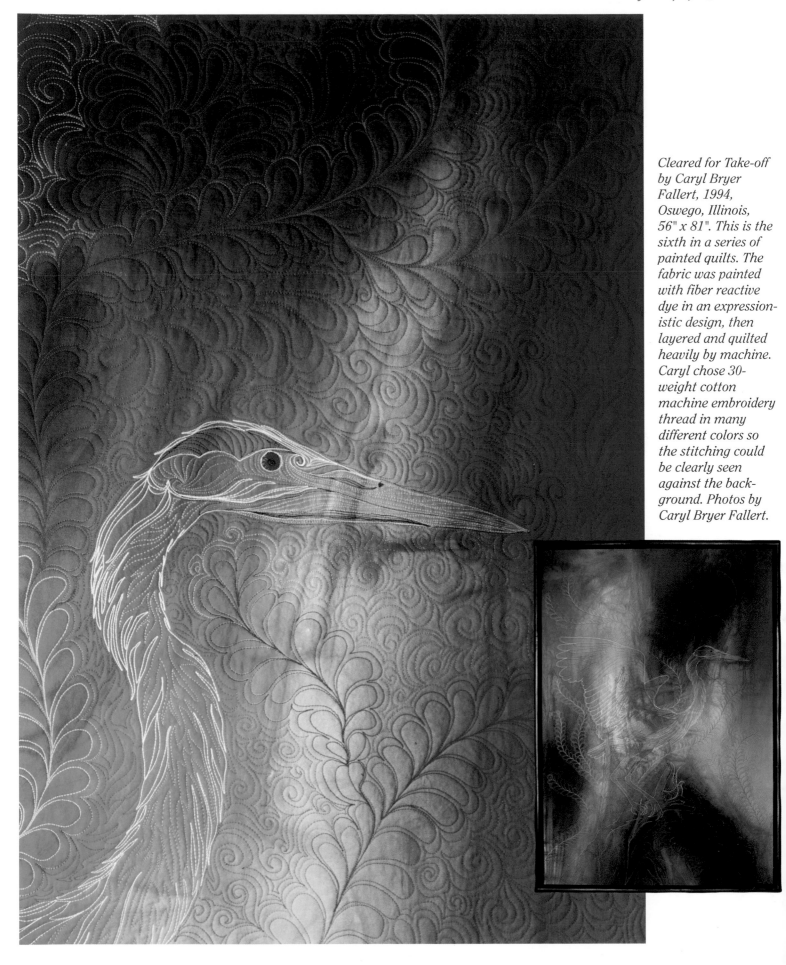

Cleared for Take-off by Caryl Bryer Fallert, 1994, Oswego, Illinois, 56" x 81". This is the sixth in a series of painted quilts. The fabric was painted with fiber reactive dye in an expressionistic design, then layered and quilted heavily by machine. Caryl chose 30-weight cotton machine embroidery thread in many different colors so the stitching could be clearly seen against the background. Photos by Caryl Bryer Fallert.

Tinderbox by Libby Lehman, 1994, Houston, Texas, 46" x 46". The base of this quilt is a traditional pieced pattern overlaid with a hand-dyed fabric that is stitched and cut away, leaving the background visible. The entire surface is embellished with rayon and metallic decorative threads stitched freehand from the top as well as from the bobbin. The luminous quality was achieved by using Stream Lamé and Sulky Sliver thread. Photos by Libby Lehman.

Faces by Elizabeth Hendricks, 1994, Seattle, Washington, 41" x 50". This quilt design developed from cutaway fabric pieces stitched onto the background, then couched, quilted, and embellished on the surface, leaving ends of the decorative threads and yarns to hang free. The faces are densely quilted with a matching DMC 50 thread. The ribbon stitching in the side and bottom borders was done freehand, using ribbon floss in the bobbin. Couched chenille yarn gives texture to the top border. Photos by Roger Schreiber.

Red, Cream, and Blue Feathered Star Variation by Debra Wagner, 1991, Cosmos, Minnesota, 60" x 60". The quilt body is five pieced feathered stars. Quilting and trapunto were added to the eagles and the borders. The quilting was done with DMC 50 cotton machine embroidery thread.

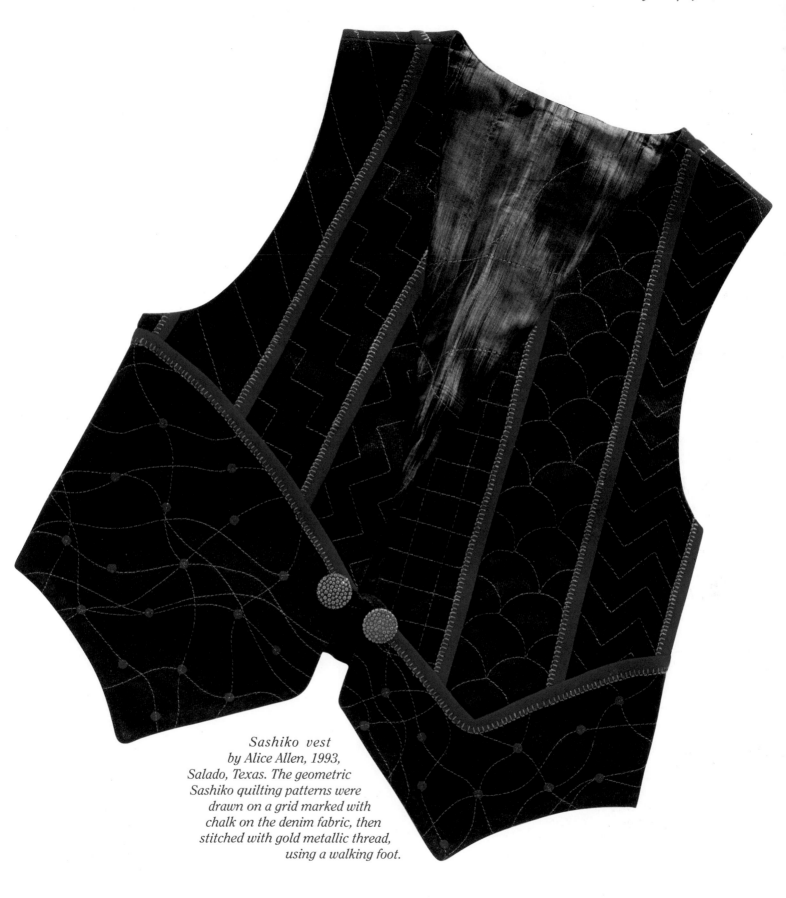

*Sashiko vest
by Alice Allen, 1993,
Salado, Texas. The geometric
Sashiko quilting patterns were
drawn on a grid marked with
chalk on the denim fabric, then
stitched with gold metallic thread,
using a walking foot.*

Detail of Antique Quilt, maker unknown, hand pieced, 1880–1920, machine quilted 1940s. This quilt belonged to Annabelle Graham Joslyn, who moved from West Plains, Missouri, to Idaho, then to the Portland, Oregon, area early in this century. She was born in the 1880s and brought the quilt top with her when she moved. The quilting is an unusual continuous pattern. Owned by Bob and Pat Smith of Newberg, Oregon; Annabelle was Bob's maternal grandmother.

Geometric Sample by Maurine Noble, 1994, Seattle, Washington. If you can't draw or think of a design to follow, a geometric fabric provides an interesting design for couching with decorative threads.

Cranes by Maurine Noble, 1994, Seattle, Washington, 19" x 19". The delicate cranes are gold braid couched with irridescent threads. The design was drawn on paper, stitched freehand through the paper with invisible nylon thread, then couched with gold braid, following the nylon thread pattern.

Detail of Chutney by Maurine Noble, 1994, Seattle, Washington. This Scrap Rail Fence was quilted with decorative satin stitches, using DMC 50 variegated thread and a walking foot. Ties were applied by machine, using Carat braid.

Detail of Scrap Double Irish Chain by Maurine Noble, 1994, Seattle, Washington. This quilt has a batik print background with scrap chain pieces; it is quilted in Sulky 30 with a twin needle and running stitch, using a walking foot. The borders were added after the quilting was completed.

Detail of Double Irish Chain, pieced by Mical Middaugh, quilted by Maurine Noble, 1993, Seattle, Washington. This Double Irish Chain was quilted in a traditional manner by diagonally stitching through the chains, then freehand stitching the continuous floral design in the open spaces.

◀ *Things That Growl in the Night by Maurine Roy, 1993, Edmonds, Washington, 38" x 50". This twisted Log Cabin was a challenge for the maker to use her brown fabrics. The quilting was done from the back side by following the design on the printed backing fabric.*

The collage of quilts surrrounding the quilt at top left are just a few of the many samples that I have made to use when I teach machine quilting classes. They were stitched with a variety of decorative threads, using both straight-line and freehand quilting techniques.

Exercise 11

Determining Tension Settings for Decorative Threads in the Bobbin

1. Prepare a 14" quilt sandwich (page 5).

2. Mark 5 horizontal lines, 2" apart, on the fabric and number them from 3 to 7 to indicate tension settings as shown below.

3. Follow the procedure on page 24 for making a tension sample but start with your tension set at 3 instead of 1, and stop at 7 instead of 9. Stitch a line for each decorative thread you would like to use. Try a few simple decorative stitches. Heavy decorative threads stitched from the bobbin look best in a very simple stitch such as a long straight stitch, an open zigzag, or a simple decorative stitch. Remember to mark the stitch length, width, and stitch pattern number on your sample for future reference.

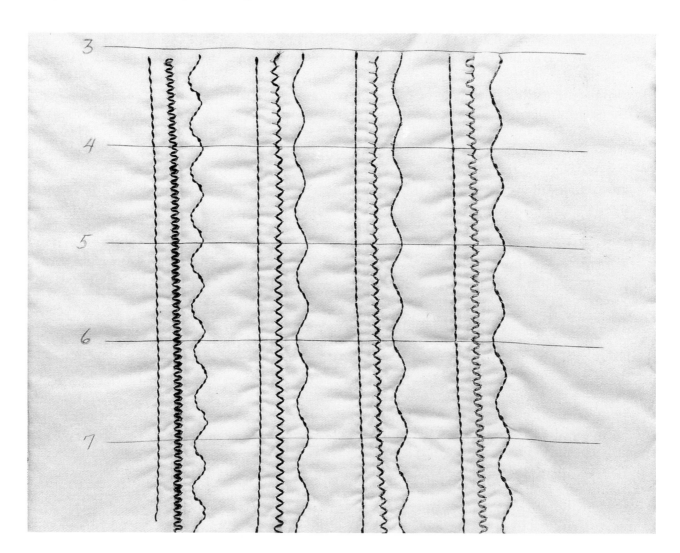

Sashiko is a decorative form of Japanese stitchery that uses a long running stitch to create grid patterns. It is traditionally done with heavy, contrasting colored thread on solid-colored fabric. If I am doing Sashiko-type quilting, I use a stronger top thread like Mettler Metrosene Plus polyester or J. & P. Coats Dual Duty Plus®, in a color to match the background fabric. Using a contrasting color and stronger thread in the top makes a more prominent break in the heavier decorative thread on the bottom, giving a look similar to that of hand stitching. If you try this and the decorative thread from the bobbin looks too loose, tighten the bobbin case screw slightly.

Decorative threads in the bobbin can also be stitched freehand by using a darning foot and dropping the feed dogs. Depending upon your machine and the thread, you may have to adjust both the bobbin and top tensions to stitch freehand and get balanced tension.

Because you are quilting from the back side of your quilt, you will usually mark your pattern or stitching line on the back side of the quilt. Mark the stitching line with the same tools you use for marking the top side.

For some quilts it may be necessary to mark a pattern or design on the front before stitching from the back. In these cases, I stitch the pattern from the top side of the quilt using invisible nylon thread and a long basting stitch. This line is clearly visible from the back side, and the decorative thread can be stitched either parallel to or on top of the basting stitch. If the decorative thread covers the basting stitches, you do not need to remove them. If the basting does show, it can be removed easily. Experimenting on a sample will again be helpful.

Using a Twin Needle

A twin needle has two needles attached to a bar on a single shank that inserts into your machine. Twin needles come in several sizes; the size on the package denotes the distance between the two needles and their size. When using a twin needle, you will use two spools of thread on the top of the machine, but only one bobbin thread. This creates two parallel lines of stitching on the top side and a zigzag stitch on the back side.

To thread the machine with two spools of thread, follow this procedure.

1. Pull the thread off the right spool pin in a clockwise direction; place the thread on the right side of the tension disk, through the normal thread guides and the right needle eye.

2. Pull the thread off the left spool in a counter-clockwise direction; place the thread on the left side of the tension disk, through the normal thread guides and the left needle eye.

When the machine is threaded carefully, in this order, the threads should not twist but should flow through the threading path easily. If threads shred or break, omit threading through the thread guide above the needle. You will need to loosen the thread tension.

The narrower set of twin needles will give you a narrow zigzag stitch on the back side of your quilt and a wider swing to a decorative stitch. If your machine has a maximum stitch width of 5mm and you use twin needles that are set 2mm apart, you can set the stitch width no wider than 3mm when using a decorative stitch. Many of the computerized sewing machines have a twin needle width control adjustment. If you have this function on your machine, be sure to use it. It will prevent broken needles.

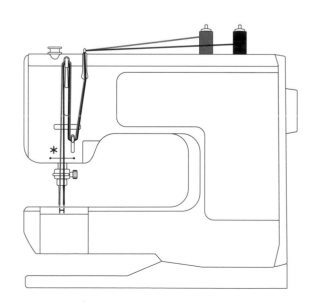

Exercise 12

Quilting with a Twin Needle

1. Prepare a 14" quilt sandwich (page 5).

2. Insert a twin needle in your machine and thread your machine with 2 contrasting threads. For this exercise, use lighter or medium-weight threads. Loosen the top tension and set it at least one number lower.

3. Attach the walking foot or engage the dual feed.

4. Stitch a straight line the length of the fabric.

5. Now select a decorative stitch. Try several different simple decorative stitches, remembering to adjust the stitch width to correspond with the width of your needles. When you are first learning, you will inevitably break a few needles—this is common.

6. If you have room on your practice piece, try some freehand quilting. Remove the walking foot, lower the feed dogs, attach the darning foot and set the stitch to a straight stitch. Experiment with different shapes and with stippling. You can use the same patterns that you used for freehand quilting with a single needle. If the left thread breaks, you need to loosen the top tension. Prepare another quilt sandwich so that you can fully explore some of the unique possibilities that a twin needle provides.

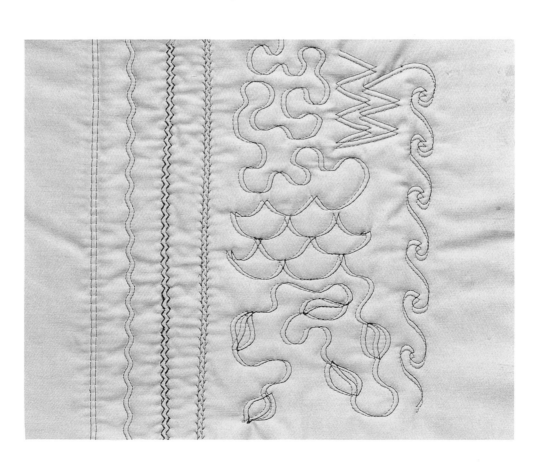

More on Twin Needles

When quilting with twin needles, you do need to tie off the threads. One method is to just begin stitching and then to pull the thread ends through to the back when you are all done and weave them into the batting of the quilt. This is a tedious chore.

I prefer to tie off with short stitches in the seam allowance. After the quilting is finished, I add borders and/or binding to the quilt. The tie-off stitches are concealed in the seam allowance of the border or binding.

Another method for tying off is to begin stitching with 8–10 short straight stitches, stitch the decorative stitch, and end with another 8–10 short straight stitches. You can change the needle position for the straight tie-off stitches to correspond with the placement of the needles at the beginning and end of the decorative stitch.

Triple needles are also available. Follow the exercise for the twin needle to experiment with a triple needle. Use a thread stand for the third spool of thread or wind two of the top threads on bobbins and place the bobbins on one spool pin. Two of the threads will have to be placed on the same side of the tension disk. Triple needles require a bit more practice, but they can be fun. I often use a stronger thread in the left needle, as it tends to break more easily than the other two.

Couching with Decorative Threads

The heavier threads that can only be used in the bobbin can also be couched onto the quilt top. Threads, yarns, braids, ribbons, or combinations of these can be twisted together and couched.

Couching is done by laying the heavy thread on the top surface and stitching over it with invisible nylon, matching, or contrasting thread. The over-stitching can be done with a zigzag, blind hem, buttonhole, straight, or any decorative stitch that will give the desired look. Some machines have a braiding foot that will guide the couching cord as you stitch over it. The braiding foot has a hole in which to insert the yarns. The foot then guides the yarns as you follow the design. It works well for long, easy lines, but if there are a lot of detailed curves in your design, an open-toe embroidery foot provides better visibility and manipulation space.

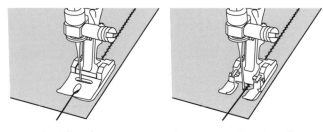

Braiding foot   Open-toe embroidery foot

Couching is often done on the quilt top *before* the top, batting, and back are pinned together. However, I do couching through the top and batting so that the batting stabilizes my stitching. It can be done on the top without batting or backing, by placing the fabric in an embroidery hoop to stabilize it. If you couch through the top and batting or through the top only, you will need to quilt through all three layers later to secure the front layers to the back.

Couching can also be stitched through the top, the batting, and the backing, if desired. Some people, however, prefer not to see the zigzag couching stitches on the back of the quilt.

The gold braid triangles on Elizabeth Hendrick's quilt on page 31 were couched onto the quilt top before the quilt was sandwiched. With the quilt top held taut in a hoop, the braid was couched with variegated metallic thread, using an open-toe embroidery foot and a narrow, open zigzag stitch.

The couching on the geometric sampler on page 41 was done with a braiding foot. The cranes were couched using an open-toe embroidery foot to allow for better visibility and maneuverability of the intricate design.

Exercise 13

Learning to Couch

1. Choose a printed fabric to follow or mark a simple pattern on a 14" square of muslin with a marking tool. Another way to mark a design for couching is to stitch the design into the quilt top and batting in invisible nylon thread, then follow the stitching line with couching thread.

2. Attach the braiding foot on your machine if you have one, or use an open-toe embroidery foot. Thread the needle with invisible nylon thread, matching, or contrasting decorative thread, and fill the bobbin with a lightweight cotton, bobbin thread or invisible nylon thread.

3. Select a heavy decorative thread, cord, yarn or braid. Hold the spool or skein in your lap. Thread the cord or yarn into the hole of the braiding foot. If you are using an open-toe embroidery foot, place the end of the cord under the foot, between the front edges.

4. Slowly stitch the cord onto the quilt sandwich with or without backing (see page 40), following a design you have drawn or a design in the fabric. You will have to adjust the width of your zigzag stitch until it just covers the cords or yarns you are using. To turn, stop with the needle in the quilt sandwich and pivot.

5. Tie off the beginning and ending threads by inserting them through a needle and weaving them through the batting of the quilt to secure them.

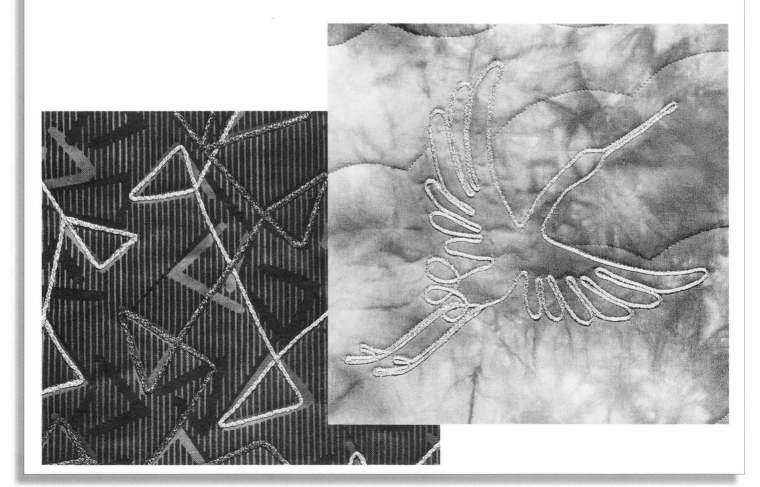

Exercise 14

Braiding Decorative Threads

You can also attach yarns, ribbons, or braids to the surface by topstitching through the quilt layers with invisible nylon or decorative thread in the needle while forming a braid or chain by crossing the yarns as you stitch.

1. Prepare a 14" quilt sandwich (page 5).

2. Attach the open-toe embroidery foot on your machine. Thread the needle with invisible nylon or decorative thread.

3. To practice, start with 24" lengths of 2 or more pieces of yarn, braid, or ribbon. Fold the pieces in half to determine the midpoints. Place the midpoints at the top of the quilt sandwich. Secure with 3, 4, or any set number of stitches, going over the yarn and stopping with the needle in the fabric.

4. Raise the presser foot, cross the yarns in front of the needle, lower the presser foot, and stitch through the cross, using the same number of stitches. Stop with the needle in the fabric. If you have a computerized machine that you can program, set the "needle down" button, program 2 or 3 straight stitches into the memory, set the stop button, and the machine does all the work for you. All you do is raise the presser foot and cross the yarns.

5. Repeat the crossing and stitching until you reach the ends of the yarn.

Planning Your Quilting

Pattern Ideas

First you must determine how and where you plan to use the quilt. A quilt you will use daily and launder often may not require lots and lots of fine quilting. Many traditional quilts are made with blank squares to allow for fancy quilting designs. A wall hanging may not be handled much but will be seen by many, so it may need more detailed quilting. Other quilts look good with stitching in-the-ditch or outline quilting, or diagonal stitching through the pieced blocks. A curved quilting line will soften and give a completely different design feeling to a geometrically pieced quilt top. Let the piecing pattern of your quilt top help you decide how to quilt it.

Often the color and pattern in the piecing make such strong statements that minimal quilting is needed. A traditionally patterned quilt top may need very traditional quilting if the fabrics used give it an "old world" look. The same pieced pattern may look entirely different when made from other fabrics and may call for a contemporary approach to the quilting.

The Double Irish Chain quilts shown on page 35 are examples of how completely different the same piecing pattern can look, and what a different feeling they evoke when quilted in dissimilar ways. The navy, turquoise, and mauve scrap quilt was quilted using a twin needle and 30-weight Sulky rayon thread. A simple running stitch adds further interest to the diagonal quilting lines. The purple and yellow quilt was quilted with a more traditional pattern using Mettler Silk Finish thread for the diagonal chains and DMC 50 for the block motifs.

It is helpful to study the quilting in quilts you admire in shows and see photographed in books and magazines. Studying them gives you ideas to incorporate into your own quilting pattern resource file. After quilting a few tops and being aware of what appeals to you in the quilts you see, you will find that quilt tops tell you how they need to be quilted. They speak to you!

Here are some things to think about when designing your quilting patterns:

- How will the quilt be used?
- Who is it for?
- Is it traditional or contemporary?
- Do you want the quilting to be an important part of the overall design, or is it there just to hold the layers together?
- How skilled at and comfortable with machine quilting are you?
- Do you have a time limitation?
- Should it be machine tied? (See page 50.)

Planning the Quilting Lines or Pattern

Here is an idea to help you get a feeling for what the quilt will look like with various quilting lines or patterns. Take a photograph of the quilt top (I use a 4" x 6" print), slide it into a clear plastic bag, and draw proposed quilting lines on the plastic bag with a felt-tipped pen. By moving the photograph to a clear space on the plastic and drawing more lines, you can explore various ideas for quilting.

Marking the Quilting Lines

Many quilts can be completely quilted without marking. For example, you do not need to mark stitching in-the-ditch, outline quilting, stippling, and straight and diagonal lines. To keep lines straight and parallel, use a quilting guide that attaches to your walking foot. If your walking foot does not take a quilting guide, you can mark lines with a marking tool to help keep lines evenly spaced.

It is necessary to mark more complex patterns. Numerous marking pens, pencils, and chalks are available. I have tried most of them and find the following to be the most useful.

Washable blue or purple marking pen. Use for intricate quilting patterns and designs that are usually marked on the quilt top before pinning. Do not mark until you are ready to quilt, since heat and time will set the lines, making them difficult or impossible to remove. Trace the pattern using a dotted line rather than a solid line, to minimize the amount of ink absorbed by the fabric and batting. To remove the marks, soak the completed quilt in cold water until the color disappears, then wash the quilt in the washing machine on a gentle cycle with lukewarm water and mild soap. Washing with soap removes the chemical from the washable ink, which does not come out with cold water alone.

Chakoner wheel marker. Use for simple designs or lines. Must be quilted immediately before the chalk disappears, as it rubs off easily. Use the white only, because the pigment in the other colors is not always removable.

Hera® marker. Use to score straight lines. Makes a crease on the fabric that is easy to follow. Mark one section at time. It leaves no residue and there is nothing to remove.

Con-Tact® self-adhesive plastic. Use for cutting shapes or templates. Peel the backing paper away to stick the template to the quilt top. Stitch around the template, remove, and reposition to stitch again. Reuse until the sticky backing is saturated with lint and will not adhere. Several templates can be cut at one time.

Tracing paper or other firm-surfaced paper. (Medical examining table paper works well.) Use for drawing or tracing a quilting pattern. Use a purple disappearing marking pen to mark a dotted line on the paper. Pin the paper pattern to the top of the quilt and stitch through the paper, working with one manageable section of the pattern at a time. Carefully tear to remove the paper after quilting. Using the disappearing marking pen leaves no unsightly ink residue.

A quick method for making multiple patterns is to trace or draw a pattern on paper with a heat transfer pen and then transfer the pattern to as many pieces of paper as the number of designs needed. Use the heat transfer pen on paper only; it leaves a permanent mark on fabric.

Continuous Pattern Designs

The pattern design you choose for machine quilting should be as continuous as possible. It is easier to stitch around the border of your quilt several times to complete a border design than to constantly start and stop to create the design. Many traditional quilting patterns are already continuous or can be slightly redesigned to make them continuous. Lay a sheet of tracing paper over an existing quilting pattern and follow the pattern lines with a pencil. Make minor changes if necessary to make the lines continuous. There are numerous books and patterns available that offer designs specifically for continuous machine quilting. See the Resource List/References on page 63.

To design a corner for a border, set a mirror at a 45° angle to the border pattern and slide the mirror along until you see a corner that pleases you.

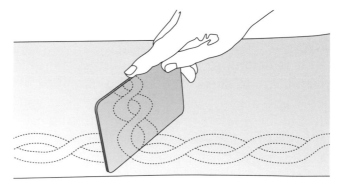

Trace the corner pattern on paper, then mark it on all four corners of your quilt. Now measure the distance between corner motifs to determine how many repeats of the border design you need and how much adjusting needs to be done to fill the space.

Allover continuous patterns such as stippling, feathers, and grid quilting are frequently used for the background. Use them to quilt a whole quilt top or just for the background in specific areas.

You can use an allover background design around an appliqué or a quilting motif, or in any area that needs to be filled in. Debra Wagner's quilt on page 32 shows a traditional stippled background surrounding the padded eagle motif. Background quilting flattens out the background, making appliqué and quilted motifs stand out.

Traditional background techniques include stippling, echo, channel, grid, clamshells, teacups, and many variations of these and other patterns. The quilted vest on page 33 illustrates Japanese Sashiko quilting patterns. Many are the same as or similar to traditional patterns; the use of heavier decorative threads makes them Sashiko style.

When all else fails, my quick and easy solution for deciding on a quilting pattern is to use a continuous patterned printed fabric for the quilt backing. I follow the pattern of the print, stitching from the back side, to get an allover quilting pattern without having to do any marking. Use the thread chosen for the top of the quilt in the bobbin. The quilt on page 36 is an example of this technique. Maurine Roy followed the lines in a bamboo print in her quilting.

Selecting the Batting

To handle the bulk of a quilt when machine quilting, it is best to use a lightweight batting. I prefer cotton batting because it rolls easily, is not as likely to beard, and is comfortable to sleep under because it breathes. Quilts made with cotton batting are flatter than those made with high-loft polyester batting, but they are soft and cuddly, and the batting shrinks to give them a wonderful traditional look. If you want a thick loft, you will need to use a polyester batting.

All battings have a finish on them to make them easier to use. The finish, often a starch, disappears when the finished quilt is washed. Many cotton battings are now needlepunched. These battings are stronger and denser, which means your quilting lines can be stitched farther apart.

A list of readily available packaged battings is shown in Table 5 on page 62. It includes the manufacturers' suggested maximum quilting distances. Battings are grouped by fiber content and listed alphabetically by manufacturer within each group. Battings from the same manufacturer are sorted by weight, from lightest to heaviest.

Many more brands of batting are available either in packages or by the yard. I chose these because they are available in most quilt shops and mail order catalogs. Washed cotton flannel can also be used as a batting. It gives warmth without loft.

Prewash or presoak cotton battings if you do not want them to shrink after quilting; follow package directions.

The process of machine quilting causes shrinkage in the length and width of the quilt. A thick batting draws the top and backing fabrics together as you stitch. This is less of a problem with a thin batting. If you need a specific size quilt, make a sample first. Make a quilt sandwich out of the quilt fabric and batting and machine quilt it as you plan to quilt the whole quilt. Measure the sample before quilting, after quilting, and after washing and drying. You can then calculate and allow for the shrinkage. This same sample also lets you try various threads and marking tools.

Keep a record of the batting and thread you use for each quilt. When you find the perfect combination, you can use it again and again.

Piecing the Batting

You may need to piece the batting for a large quilt. Use your sewing machine to piece cotton batting. The following method creates a flat join that cannot be detected in the finished quilt.

1. Attach your walking foot and thread the needle with white or ecru cotton thread. Set the stitch for a 5mm-wide sewn-out zigzag or running stitch with a .75mm stitch length.

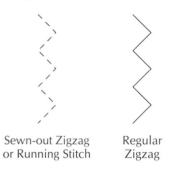

Sewn-out Zigzag   Regular
or Running Stitch   Zigzag

2. Overlap the edges of the pieces to be joined and make a clean, straight cut with a rotary cutter and ruler.
3. Remove the strips you trimmed off and hold the 2 pieces snugly together as you sew the cut edges together, catching both pieces of the batting as the needle moves from side to side.

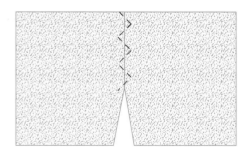

Piece thicker polyester battings by hand in the following manner:

1. Overlap the edges of the pieces to be joined; make a clean cut with a rotary cutter and ruler. On both pieces, separate the batting into two layers 1" from the cut edges.

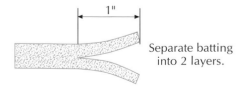

Separate batting into 2 layers.

2. Use scissors to trim the top layer of separated batting 1" from the edge on batting piece #1. Trim the bottom layer of the separated batting, also 1" from the edge, on batting piece #2.
3. Overlap the cut edges and whip together by hand, first on the top side and then on the bottom side, using matching thread. This makes a smooth, ridgeless join.

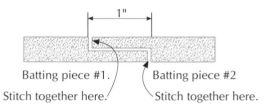

Batting piece #1.   Batting piece #2
Stitch together here.   Stitch together here.

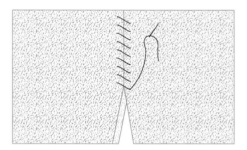

Preparing the Layers

Preparing the three layers of your quilt for machine quilting is probably the most important part of the whole process. The first project you quilt should be a size that is easy to handle.

1. Cut the backing fabric and batting so that they extend 2" to 4" beyond the quilt-top edges. Press to remove all wrinkles. Fold the backing and batting in quarters and mark the center point with pins.
2. Spread the backing out on a table, wrong side up, and clip it to the edge of the table every 10" to 15" with 2" binder clips (available in most office supply stores). If the quilt is smaller than the table, clip one side and one end to the table edges and tape the remaining side and end to the tabletop. If the quilt is larger than the table, start with the center of the quilt in the center of the table and clip the backing all around the tabletop.
3. Lay the batting on top of the backing, matching center pins. Remove the pin from the backing. Remove the binder clips one at a time and reclip with batting.

4. Match the center of the quilt top with the center of the batting, remove the center pin, smooth out the top, and reclip with the quilt top. Make sure the batting and backing still extend evenly beyond the quilt top. The 3 layers should be smooth and taut, but not stretched or distorted.

5. Begin pinning, using 1" (#1) safety pins and catching all 3 layers of the quilt sandwich. Place the pins where you won't be stitching. Work from the center out, pinning at 3" (polyester batting) to 4" (cotton batting) intervals. Leave the pins open. A quilt with polyester batting needs more pins than one with cotton batting because cotton fabric shifts more with polyester batting.

6. Close the pins using a grapefruit spoon or a Kwik Klip. The pin catches in one of the notches on the grapefruit spoon or the Kwik Klip. Using a tool to close the pins prevents very sore fingertips.

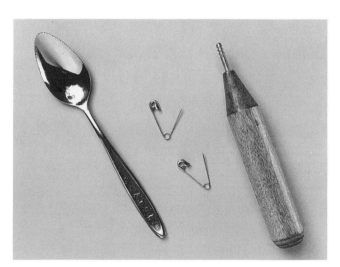

The QuilTak™

The QuilTak is a relatively new tool. It forces plastic tacks, instead of safety pins, through the quilt sandwich to hold the layers together.

The normal method for using the QuilTak is to push the needle from the front to the back. This leaves a plastic end on both sides of the quilt.

For better visibility, a tighter hold on the layers, and easier removal, I use the following method to baste the layers together with a QuilTak.

1. Pin the backing, batting, and quilt top one layer at a time to builder's insulation board mounted on a wall, removing the pins from the previous layer as you pin the next one. Use long straight pins and place them on an angle, in vertical rows 10" to 12" apart.

2. Begining in the center, tack through all three layers by pushing the needle into the layers, then back through the layers to the top surface before shooting the tack. Use a spoon held in your other hand to stop the needle and push it back to the top side. Both of the plastic ends will be on the front side.

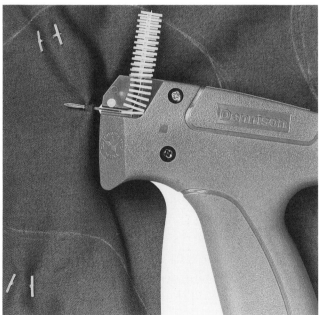

3. Working out from the center of the quilt, make a tack every 3" to 4", always being careful not to tack a pleat into the quilt.

4. As you quilt, or after you complete the quilting, cut one plastic end of the tack to remove it. Be careful not to clip the quilt.

Quilting the Quilt

When the quilt sandwich is securely pinned or tacked, you are ready to begin machine quilting. As you quilt, you may need to remove pins or tacks that are in your way. Tape a disposable plastic cup to the front edge of your machine table, to the right of your machine. As you remove safety pins, leave them open and deposit them in the plastic cup. The pins are then ready to use in your next quilt.

The basic steps for machine quilting are:

1. Stitch the design lines in the quilt to secure the quilt sandwich. These would be horizontal, vertical, or diagonal lines that can be stitched at regular intervals, such as along the sashing or seams between blocks. Beginning at the center of the top edge for straight lines and at one of the top corners for diagonal lines, stitch the full length of the line. Continue stitching at regular intervals in one direction until half of the quilt is stitched.

2. Turn the quilt 180° and stitch the other half of the lengthwise lines at the same intervals in the opposite direction. *Working from the center of the quilt to the outside edges keeps shifting to a minimum.*

3. Repeat the same process, starting at the center side edges and stitching horizontal lines out from the center in both directions.

Look at the ABC appliqué quilt below and follow the steps as we work through the quilting sequence for this quilt.

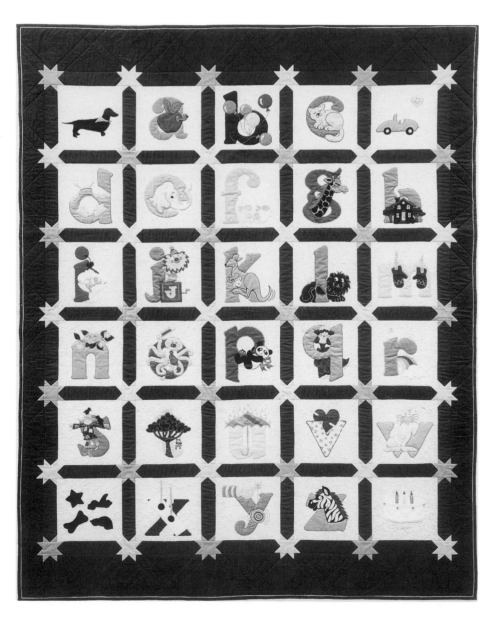

1. The first step is to stitch in-the-ditch of the sashing around each square. Roll the long right-hand edge of the quilt toward the center, stopping at the C block. If the roll will not stay tight, secure it with a bicycle clip, a plastic clip, or safety pins at 20" intervals. Set your stitch length to 10–11 stitches per inch and remember to begin and end each line of stitching by tying off with 8–10 small stitches. Beginning on the top right side of the B block, stitch from star to star.

2. *Without cutting threads*, move the needle to the top right side of the F block and stitch from star to star. Continue in this manner, stitching on the right sides of blocks K, P, U, and Y.

3. Cut the thread and move the quilt so this procedure can be repeated on the other side of the sashing, the left sides of blocks C, G, L, Q, V, and Z. Unroll the quilt as necessary to reveal the next row of blocks. Repeat on both sides of the sashing between blocks until all vertical lines on the right half of the quilt are machine quilted.

4. Turn the quilt around so that the letters are now upside down and again roll the right half of the quilt to the center. Repeat steps 1, 2, and 3, beginning on the right side of the upside down Y block. Now you are working from the bottom of the quilt to the top. When all the vertical lines are quilted, carefully cut the threads between the blocks.

5. Turn the quilt sideways and repeat steps 1, 2, 3, and 4 to quilt the horizontal lines. When you are done, you will have stitched around each block in 4 separate segments. Trim the threads between the blocks and quilt the borders.

6. I outlined and detailed the appliquéd shapes with a freehand straight stitch (darning foot on, feed dogs dropped), using nylon thread in the needle and in the bobbin because of the many fabric and thread colors. The stippling thread is a light gray DMC 50 thread which blends well with the mottled background fabric.

Quilt most quilt tops in this same sequence. When the main quilting lines are diagonal, as in the Double Irish Chain quilts on page 35, roll the quilt to the center from the corners, instead of the sides. It can be difficult to squeeze this much bulk into the opening in your machine. I once successfully quilted a 124" x 124" bedspread in one piece. It wasn't easy; lightweight cotton batting made it possible. In addition to being thinner, cotton batting holds a roll better than polyester batting.

Quilt-As-You-Go Method for Large Quilts

You may also quilt a queen- or king-sized quilt in 2 or 3 sections for ease of handling. Assemble the sections in the "quilt-as-you-go" method.

1. Quilt each section, leaving at least 1" unstitched along the edges to be joined.

2. Sew the top fabrics of the 2 sections together and press the seam allowances to one side.

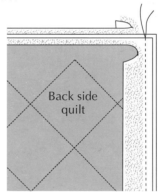

3. Trim the batting sections so that they butt together on or near the seam line. Use a whip stitch to join the 2 pieces of batting together. An alternate method is to catch the batting in the seam when you sew the top fabrics together and then trim the excess. This works best with lightweight battings.

4. Smooth one piece of the backing over the batting joint. Turn under the seam allowance of the other piece of backing and lay it over the raw edge of the first piece.

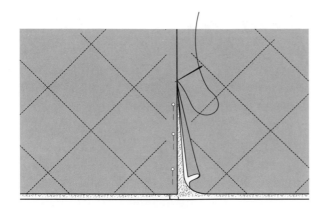

5. Stitch the seam by hand using a blind stitch, or on the machine with a blind hem stitch, using a short stitch and a narrow zigzag to just barely catch the fabric. Do not use a blind hem foot. I use an edge-stitch foot for this step.

A Final Note

When you machine quilt a project that will take several hours to complete, don't crouch over the machine for long stretches of time. Use an oven timer to remind you to get up and stretch.

An adjustable secretary-type chair can help, allowing you to change position and height. Adjust the chair to its highest position and set the timer for 30 minutes. Quilt until the timer buzzes and stop. Get up and do a short chore like making the bed, starting a load of laundry, or doing 50 jumping jacks.

Return to your machine, lower your chair a notch, and reset the timer for another 30 minutes. Continue in this manner all day if necessary. When the chair gets too low, reset it to the highest position. You will become very innovative in your "break" activities as your neck and back begin to show the strain of being hunched over your machine. Your body will be willing to work longer if you give it frequent breaks.

The way you handle the quilt also makes a difference. The quilt roll in the opening of your machine needs to be supported as you stitch. Try holding the roll by supporting it over your left shoulder. As the roll moves closer to the machine, smooth the quilt out and check on the underside for tucks with your right hand.

Tying a Quilt by Machine

Tying is a good choice when you want to use an extra heavy or lofty batting. Thicker battings are much more difficult to quilt by machine or by hand than they are to tie by machine. A tie holds the layers together and can be made with yarn, ribbon, thread, or any material you would like to use. You may want to add a decorative tie, just for looks, to a quilt that has been hand or machine quilted. The tie can be utilitarian or decorative, flat or dimensional, colorful or almost invisible.

You can easily tie a quilt by machine in a number of ways. Pin or tack the quilt for tying the same way you pinned or tacked it for ma-

chine quilting. See pages 46-47. Then decide where you want to place the ties. The type of batting you are using may determine placement. For example, if you are using batting that needs to be quilted every 3", you must place a tie every 3" or closer. If the batting only needs to be quilted every 6", you can place a tie every 6". Ties can be placed at the intersections of blocks, in the middle of blocks, or randomly.

When using yarn or ribbon for the ties, you may want to precut lengths for ease of handling. Determine the length to cut by making a sample first. The length will vary depending on whether you tie a single knot, an overhand knot, or a bow.

Exercise 15

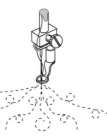

Tying a Quilt

☐ **1.** Prepare a 14" quilt sandwich (page 5).

☐ **2.** Thread your sewing machine with invisible nylon thread on the top spool and in the bobbin, drop the feed dogs, attach the darning foot, and set on a straight stitch.

☐ **3.** Place 1 length of yarn or ribbon at the center near the top edge of the quilt sandwich. Stitch across the center of the yarn or ribbon length while moving the quilt slowly forward, back, and forward again. This secures the yarn in place through the layers of the quilt.

☐ **4.** Lift the presser foot and move the quilt to the next tie position; do not cut the threads between the ties until the whole process is completed. Repeat the stitching with another length of yarn or ribbon.

☐ **5.** When you have stitched all of the ties in place, tie each one in a bow, a single knot, a square knot, or an overhand knot.

☐ **6.** Beginning with the first tie, stitch around each knot or bow twice. For the overhand knot, hold the tails out of the way and stitch through one side of the knot, then the other side. This makes the knot stand up instead of lying flat on the surface of the quilt. When you have secured all the knots or bows, clip the threads on the front and back of the quilt.

> *Tip:* If the knot is bulky, hold the presser foot bar halfway up and stitch around the knot. Don't lift the needle bar all the way up because you need the thread tension.

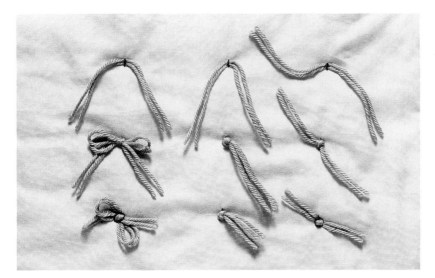

To embellish a project in just one easy step, tie a length of ribbon into a bow, place it on the quilt, and stitch a circle around the knot as shown.

Exercise 16

Tacking a Quilt

Another method of tying is to machine tack or embroider the layers of the quilt together.

☐ *1.* Prepare another quilt sandwich or use the one from Exercise 15 if you have room.

☐ *2.* Put the walking foot on your machine and thread the needle with decorative thread.

☐ *3.* Set the machine for a wide zigzag and 0 stitch length and stitch several times in one place. Without cutting the threads, move to another spot and again take several stitches in one place. Cut the threads between tacks after all have been stitched.

> *Tip:* Some computerized sewing machines have a pre-programmed button sew-on stitch that works great for tacking.

☐ *4.* Try some of the decorative stitches on your machine. Select a decorative stitch and stitch one complete pattern. Without cutting the threads, move to another spot and repeat the stitch. Cut the threads between stitches after all have been stitched.

☐ *5.* You may also stitch a motif like a heart, flower, leaf, or any other shape. Use a straight stitch or a zigzag, and your darning foot. A straight stitch will give you a single line motif. A zigzag stitch will create a satin stitch as you move the quilt to draw a motif. The needle will swing from side to side, so drawing in zigzag is much like drawing with a calligraphy pen. The width of the pen point is like the width of the zigzag swing. Practice drawing a heart by moving the fabric forward and backward, then by moving the fabric from side to side. The hearts will look different because of the direction of the swing of the needle. If you want to fill in the heart, move the quilt sandwich sideways within the heart outline, and the zigzag stitch will fill the heart center. For this type of tack, thread the bobbin and top spool with the same colored thread so the design looks the same on the front and back. A lightweight cotton embroidery thread looks good.

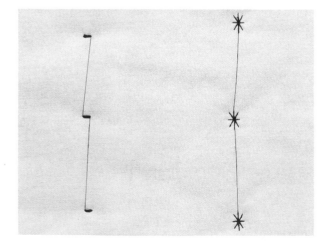

Finishing Techniques

The edges of most quilts are finished with binding. However, there are many acceptable finishing methods. My favorite resource for finishing ideas is Mimi Dietrich's *Happy Endings*, published by That Patchwork Place. The techniques included here are my favorites, French double-fold binding below, and stitch-and-turn finishing on page 55.

French Double-Fold Binding

When you have finished quilting you are ready to attach the binding. It is important to have a straight, even edge on which to stitch the binding. Trim the batting and backing even with the edges of the quilt top using a rotary cutter and ruler. Be sure the corners are square. If the quilt has a border, use the inside seam of the last border as a guide when cutting the outside edge.

To determine how wide to cut double-fold binding strips, multiply the finished width by 3, then double this amount (6 x finished width). For a ½" *finished* binding, cut strips 3" wide (½" for the seam allowance, ½" for the front of the quilt, and ½" for the back of the quilt, multiplied by 2). The only exception to this rule is a ¼"-wide finished binding, for which you should allow 7 x the finished width or 1¾". The extra ¼" provides the additional fabric needed to cover the edge of the batting with the very narrow binding.

The binding strips can be straight grain or bias cut. If the outside edge of the quilt is curved, scalloped, or anything other than straight, cut the binding on the bias so it bends easily to fit the quilt edge.

To cut straight-grain binding strips:

Cut the required number of 3"-wide strips across the width of the fabric. You will need enough strips to go around the perimeter of the quilt plus at least 12" for seams and mitered corners. To be safe, always add a few extra inches.

To cut bias binding strips:

1. Fold a square of fabric in half diagonally.

OR

Fold a ½-yard piece of fabric as shown in the diagrams at right, paying careful attention to the location of the lettered corners.

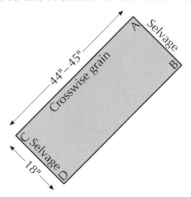

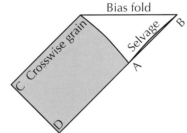

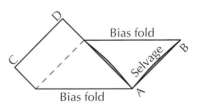

2. Cut strips 3" wide (for ½" binding), cutting perpendicular to the folds as shown.

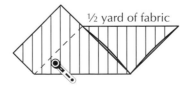

To attach binding:

1. With right sides together, sew strips end to end to make one long piece of binding. Press the seams open.

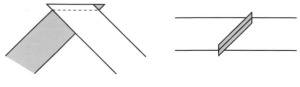

Joining bias strips

If you cut strips on the straight grain, join strips at right angles and stitch across the corner as shown. Trim excess fabric.

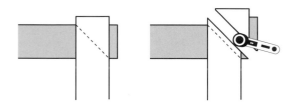

Joining straight-cut strips

2. Fold the strip in half lengthwise, wrong sides together, and press.

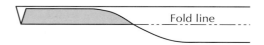

3. Starting part way in from the corner along one edge, lay the binding on the quilt top with raw edges even. Attach a walking foot and stitch the binding to the quilt, leaving at least a 6" "tail" of binding free at the start. The seam allowance should equal the desired finished width of the binding (in this case ½").

4. Stop stitching exactly ½" (or your binding width) from the corner. Pivot the quilt and stitch out to and off the edge of the corner at a 45° angle.

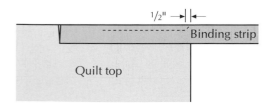

5. Fold the binding over the stitched angle, then fold it back onto itself so the raw edges of the binding and the quilt are even along the next edge. Begin stitching at the corner using an accurate seam allowance. Remember, if your finished binding is ½", use a ½" seam allowance.

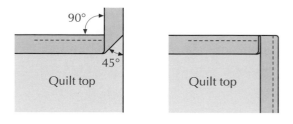

6. Continue stitching and mitering corners around the remaining edges of the quilt. Stitch to within 8" of the starting tail. Join the tails using one of the following two methods:

   - *To overlap the tails*, unfold the beginning tail, trim the end at a 45° angle, fold the end under ¼", and press. Unfold the ending tail and lay it over the beginning tail. Using scissors, carefully cut the ending tail off at a 45° angle, leaving about 1" of fabric overlapping the beginning tail. Fold the bindings in half again and finish the seam.

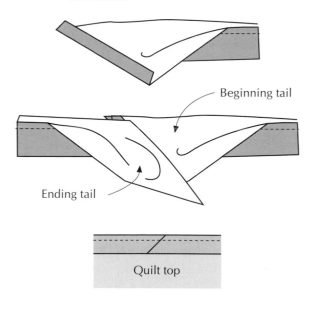

- *To seam the tails* with a straight seam, cut the 2 tails so that they overlap about 4". Unfold them. With right sides together, pin the tails together to determine where the seam should go. Stitch the seam; trim seam allowance to ¼" and press open. Refold the binding and finish stitching it in place.

Quilt top

7. Fold the binding over to the back of the quilt and pin the folded edge in place, covering the machine stitching. The corners will form a miter as they are turned. To distribute the bulk of the fabric in the corners evenly, reverse the binding fold on the corner, so the fold on the top side goes one way and fold on the back side goes the other way. Blindstitch in place, making sure the stitches do not show on the front.

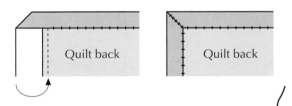

Quilt back   Quilt back

Tip: To stitch the binding entirely by machine, attach the binding to the back side of the quilt, following the steps above, then fold the binding over to the front side and topstitch in place by machine. Be sure to cover the first line of stitching with the folded edge of the binding.

Stitch-and-Turn Finishing

In this method, you finish the edges of the quilt *before* quilting. This is not as acceptable a finish as a binding, but it saves time and works well for some projects.

1. Cut the quilt backing and batting so that they extend 1" to 2" beyond the outer edges of the quilt top. Press to remove all creases and wrinkles.

2. Begin layering with the batting. Spread the batting on the tabletop, smoothing out any wrinkles. Place the backing, right side up, on top of the batting. Then place the quilt top, right side down, on top of the backing. Use 2" binder clips to secure the layers to the table one at a time.

3. Use long straight pins to pin all 3 layers together. Place the pins at right angles to the outside edges of the quilt.

4. Beginning on one side about 12" from the corner, stitch the layers together around the outside edges, using a walking foot and stitching ¼" from the raw edges of the quilt top. Take short stitches 1" before and 1" after each corner. Stitch to within 20" of the starting point.

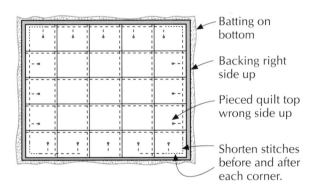

Batting on bottom

Backing right side up

Pieced quilt top wrong side up

Shorten stitches before and after each corner.

5. Backstitch 3 or 4 stitches, change the stitch length to a basting stitch, and continue stitching to the starting point; backstitch 3 or 4 stitches.

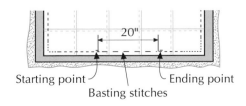

20"

Starting point — Ending point
Basting stitches

6. Press the seam allowance of the quilt top toward the body of the quilt along the basting stitches only. Set the machine stitch length back to normal and stitch the batting and backing together just outside the pressed seam allowance along the basted section.

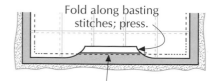

Fold along basting stitches; press.

Stitch backing and batting together next to pressed fold, using regular stitch length.

7. Trim the excess batting and backing to ½" from the stitching line, tapering the corners.
8. Remove the basting stitches and turn the quilt right side out through the opening. Carefully ease the corners into points.
9. Pin the opening closed and topstitch with a walking foot ¼" or less from the outside edge, all around the quilt.
10. Baste with safety pins to prepare for quilting.

Labeling Your Quilt

It is important to label your quilt with information about the maker, the design, the date, the place, whom the quilt was made for, and so on. You can easily work this information into the background quilting as shown below, or it can be included on a label made especially for the quilt and stitched on the back of the quilt.

If you want your signature to be inconspicuous, embroider your name and the date on the quilt in the corner or in the binding with matching thread.

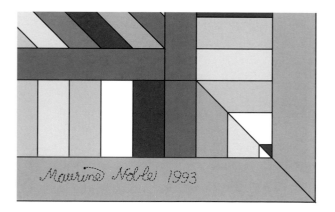

Table 1
Lightweight Threads—Threaded through the Needle

Brand Name	Fiber Content	Weight	Meters/ Yards	Suggested Needles	Notes
Invisible Monofilament	nylon or polyester	.004mm	440 and 1500 yards	Sharp or denim 70/10, 80/12 quilting 75/11	Lightweight and fine. Use with multicolor quilts or when you want an invisible line. Can be used in bobbin. Available in clear or smoke.
DMC 50	cotton	100/2	500 meters	Sharp or denim 70/10 or 80/12, quilting 75/11	Lightweight machine-embroidery thread. Excellent for stippling or heavily quilted areas. Not advisable for children's quilts, or for minimal stitching on quilts.
Madeira Cotona	cotton	80, 50, and 30	220 yards	Sharp or denim 70/10 or 80/12, quilting 75/11	3 weights of good quality machine-embroidery thread.
Mettler Machine Embroidery	cotton	60/2	200 and 1000 meters	Sharp or denim 70/10 or 80/12, quilting 75/11	Lightweight; also good for heavily quilted areas. Good choice for bobbin thread to use with other lightweight threads.
Mettler Silk Finish	cotton	50/3	150 and 500 meters	Sharp or denim 70/10 or 80/12, quilting 75/11 or 90/14	My personal favorite for stitching in-the-ditch, diagonal lines, bobbin thread and piecing quilt tops.
J. & P. Coats Dual Duty Plus Extra Fine	cotton-covered polyester	—	350 yards	Sharp or denim 70/10 or 80/12, quilting 75/11 or 90/14	Good choice for some older machines that will not stitch with the fine, lightweight threads.

Bobbin Threads

The following may also be used in the needle when you need an extra-strong lightweight thread.

Brand Name	Fiber Content	Weight	Meters/ Yards	Suggested Needles	Notes
Madeira Bobbinfil	polyester	—	500 meters		Available in white only.
Sew-Art Sew-Bob Bobbin Thread	nylon	—	1500 yards		Available in black and white only.
YLI Lingerie & Bobbin Thread	nylon	—	1200 yards		Available in black and white only.
Trusew	polyester	—	1000 yards		Available in black and white only.
Mettler Metrolene	polyester	—	2000 meters		Available in colors. Semitransparent.

Table 2
Decorative Threads—Threaded through the Needle

Brand Name	Fiber Content	Weight	Meters/ Yards	Suggested Needles	Notes
Metallics					
Madeira Metallic	metallic	—	200 meters	80/12 metafil or 80/12, 90/14 topstitch	Good-quality metallic. Easy to use.
Madeira Super Twist	metallic	—	200 meters	80/12 metafil or 80/12, 90/14 topstitch	Several fine threads twisted together. Gives special texture and a sparkle effect. Shreds easily. Use suggested needles.
Madeira FS 2/2	metallic	—	1100 yards	75/11, 90/14 embroidery, 80/12 metafil or 80/12, 90/14 topstitch	Blend of two threads, metallic and black. Gives a subtle texture. Easy to use.
Madeira Jewel	polyester	—	100 meters	80/12 metafil or 80/12, 90/14 topstitch	Hologram effect.
Prizm Hologram	metallic polyester	—	164 yards	80/12 metafil or 80/12, 90/14 topstitch	Multifaceted tinsel thread.
Stream Lamé Tinsel	mylar	—	135 yards	80/12 metafil or 80/12, 90/14 topstitch	Metallic, opalescent, wet look. Easy to use, flat ribbonlike, and highly reflective.
Sulky Metallic Embroidery Thread	metallic	—	165 yards or 1000 yards	80/12 metafil or 80/12, 90/14 topstitch	Good-quality metallic.
Sulky Sliver Metallic	mylar	—	250 yards	80/12 metafil or 80/12, 90/14 topstitch	Thin, flat, ribbonlike film, highly reflective. Easy to use.
J. & P. Coats Metallic	metallic	—	200 yards	80/12 metafil or 80/12, 90/14 topstitch	Shreds easily. Use suggested needles.
YLI Fine Metallic	metallic	—	250 yards	75/11, 90/14 embroidery, 80/12 metafil or 80/12, 90/14 topstitch	Smooth and easy to use.
Rayon					
Madeira	rayon	40 30	200 meters 150 meters	75/11, 90/14 embroidery, 80/12 metafil or 80/12, 90/14 topstitch	Fine, silky luster. Easy to use.
Sulky	rayon	40 30	250 yards 180 meters	75/11, 90/14 embroidery, 80/12 metafil or 80/12, 90/14 topstitch	Fine, silky luster. Easy to use.

Decorative Threads—Threaded through the Needle (continued)

Brand Name	Fiber Content	Weight	Meters/ Yards	Suggested Needles	Notes
Silks					
Tire	silk	—	100 meters	75/11 or 90/14 embroidery	Easy to use; similar in sheen to rayon, but more expensive.
Kanawawa Silk Stitch	silk	—		75/11 or 90/14 embroidery	Easy to use; similar in sheen to rayon, but more expensive.
Cotton and Polyester Threads					
Mettler Quilting	cotton	40/3	500 yards	80/12 or 90/14 topstitch	Creates a bold, heavy line. Good for Shashiko quilting and embroidery.
Mettler Cordonnet	polyester	30/3	150 meters	90/14 topstitch	Heavier than quilting thread, same effect.
YLI Jeanstitch	polyester	30/3	150 meters	90/14 topstitch	Same as Mettler Cordonnet, but available in larger spools.
Madeira Burmilana or Sew-Art Renaissance	30% wool 70% acrylic	—	100 yards	90/14 topstitch	Looks like crewel yarn.
Madeira Tanne	cotton	30	714 yards	80/12 or 90/14 topstitch	Similar to Mettler Cordonnet and Jeanstitch but slightly lighter weight. Thread used in "Cleared for Takeoff" on page 29 by Caryl Bryer Fallert.
Mettler Machine Embroidery	cotton	30	219 yards	80/12 or 90/14 topstitch	Same as Madeira Tanne.

Table 3
Decorative Threads for the Bobbin or Couching

Brand Name	Fiber Content	Weight	Meters/Yards	Notes
Madeira Glamour	metallic	—	100 meters	Soft, heavyweight metallic. Beautiful, bold line.
YLI Candelight	metallic	—	75 yards	Same look as Glamour.
Madeira Decor	rayon	—	200 meters	Plied (untwisted) heavyweight. Lovely sheen from plied threads.
YLI Designer 6	rayon	—	150 yards	Plied heavyweight. Very similar to Decor.
DMC Pearl Cotton	cotton	3 5 8	balls or skeins	Soft luster, tightly twisted. Lightest 8 weight can be used on the top with a 90/14 topstitch needle.
Pearl Crown Rayon	rayon		100 yards	Heavy, twisted. Rich, lustrous sheen.
Ribbon Floss™	rayon metallic		40 yards 20 yards	Use in bobbin or couch on top. Flat, soft braided ribbon flows easily through bobbin, giving a rich, lustrous sheen.
Madeira Carat	rayon and metallic	2mm and 4mm width	5 yards or 50 meter roll	Flat braid. Beautiful for couching or tying.
Kreinik Braid	metallic	#8 fine #16 medium #32 heavy	5 or 10 meters	Couches beautifully, also works in bobbin.

Table 4
Needles

Type	Sizes	Uses
Universal	60/8 to 120/20	Ball point for all woven and knit fabrics, pushes through an opening in the weave of the fabric. I mention this needle only because it is widely used. I do not use it for piecing or quilting because it is not sharp enough and often causes batting to punch through quilt backing. There are much better choices available.
Denim/Jeans	70/10 to 110/18	Sharper point for cleaner penetration of fabric. One of my three choices for piecing and quilting is this needle in a size 70/10 or 80/12. Blue dot on needle.
Sharp Microtex	60/8 to 90/14	Extra sharp point for perfectly straight stitches and microfibers. Also a favorite of mine for piecing and quilting in 70/10 or 80/12. Purple dot on needle.
Quilting	75/11 and 90/14	Special taper to the point to prevent damage to fabric when stitching through multiple layers of seam allowances (green dot on needle). I use this needle or one of the two immediately above as a sharp needle to piece and quilt with nondecorative threads.
Embroidery	75/11 and 90/14	Special scarf and larger eye to prevent shredding and breakage of metallic and other machine-embroidery threads (red dot on needle). My first choice for metallic and rayon threads. Begin with the smaller needle because it makes a smaller hole in the quilt; progress to the larger size if problems occur. If thread continues to break, use an 80/12 Metafil or 90/14 Topstitch needle.
Metafil	80/12	Specialized larger eye and scarf to prevent stripping and fraying of threads. Good for metallics and rayons.
Metallica	80/12	Comparable to Metafil.
Topstitch (System 130N)	80/12 to 110/18	Extra sharp with an extra large eye to accommodate heavier threads. Allows some heavier and rough-textured threads to flow easily through the large eye. Topstitch, Metafil, and Metallica usually solve problems if embroidery needles do not work for you. Once the plastic needle box is removed from the cardboard backing, the only way to identify these needles is by System 130N printed on the box; the name Topstitch is not on the box.
Twin Embroidery Needle	2.0/75 and 3.0/75	Use twin embroidery needles when using rayon threads. 2.0 and 3.0 is the distance between the two needles, 75 is the needle size. Twin needles are available in several other sizes, but they are Universal needles.
Twin Metallica Needle	2.5/80	Use for metallic threads.
Triple Needle	2.5/80 and 3.0/80	Three needles on a single shaft, sews three lines of stitching at once. 2.5 and 3.0 is the distance between the two outside needles. Interesting effects can be achieved with this needle, using cotton threads.

Table 5
Battings

Brand Name	Fiber Content	Quilting Distance	Comments
Fairfield Cotton Classic	80% cotton/ 20% polyester	2"–3"	Lightweight and flat. Can be divided in half for an even thinner layer. I like to use half a layer in clothing.
Fairfield Soft Touch	cotton	2"	Needlepunched, bleached white, very soft, excellent drape.
Hobbs Heirloom Cotton	80% cotton/ 20% polyester	3"	Lightly needlepunched.
Hobbs Organic Cotton	cotton	3"	Needlepunched, available with and without scrim.
Mountain Mist Blue Ribbon Cotton	cotton	1½"–2"	Like old-fashioned cotton batting.
Mountain Mist Cotton Choice	cotton	6"–8"	Needlepunched, bleached white. This is a good choice for quilts with white backgrounds.
Warm & Natural	cotton	10"	Needlepunched.
Warm & Natural	wool	10"	Needlepunched.
Hobbs Wool	wool	3"	Resin bonded, washable.
Fairfield Poly-Fil Low-Loft	polyester	2"–3"	Considered "standard" weight for polyester batting.
Fairfield Poly-Fil Traditional	polyester	2"–3"	Lightly needlepunched, slightly heavier.
Fairfield Poly-Fil High-Loft	polyester	2"–3"	Thicker for higher loft.
Hobbs Thermore	polyester	6"	Needlepunched, lightweight.
Hobbs Poly-Down & Poly-Down DK	polyester	3"	Both considered "standard" weight for polyester batting. Poly-Down DK is dark gray for darker quilts. Bearding is not as noticeable.
Mountain Mist Quilt-Light	polyester	2"	Lightest-weight polyester batting.
Mountain Mist Regular	polyester	3"	Considered "standard" weight for polyester batting.
Mountain Mist Fatt Batt	polyester	4"	Thicker for higher loft.
Mountain Mist Comfort Loft	polyester	5"	Thin needlepunched batting. Layer to the weight and loft you desire (3 layers = 1"). Layers adhere to prevent shifting.

Resource List/References

If you don't have access to a variety of threads, the following are some supply sources. Call or write for a catalog.

Creative Stitches
230 West 1700 S
Salt Lake City, UT 84115
(800) 748-5144

Sew Art International
P. O. Box 1244
Bountiful, UT 84011
(800) 231-2787

Speed Stitch
3113-D Broadpoint Drive
Harbor Heights, FL 33983
(813) 629-3199
(800) 874-4115

Things Japanese (silk only)
9805 NE 116th Street, Suite 7160
Kirkland, WA 98034
(206) 821-2287

Treadleart
25834 Narbonne Avenue
Lomita, CA 90717
(213) 534-5122

Web of Thread (most complete variety of
  decorative threads)
3240 Lone Oak Road, Suite 124
Paducah, KY 42003
(502) 554-8185
(800) 955-8185 (orders only)

Books

Allen, Alice. *Sashiko Made Simple*. Aurora, Ill.: Bernina of America, 1992.

Dietrich, Mimi. *Happy Endings: Finishing the Edges of Your Quilt*. Bothell, Wash.: That Patchwork Place, 1987.

Fanning, Robbie, and Tony Fanning. *The Complete Book of Machine Quilting*, 2d ed. Radnor, Pa.: Chilton Book Co., 1994.

Fons, Marianne. *Fine Feathers: A Quilter's Guide to Customizing Traditional Feather Quilting Designs*. Lafayette, Calif.: C&T Publishing, 1988.

Hargrave, Harriet. *Heirloom Machine Quilting*, rev. ed. Lafayette, Calif.: C&T Publishing, 1990.

Joanna, Barbara. *Continuous Curve Quilting*. Menlo Park, Calif.: Pride of the Forest, 1980.

Marston, Gwen, and Joe Cunningham. *Quilting With Style*. Paducah, Ky.: American Quilters Society, 1993.

McDowell, Ruth B. *Pattern on Pattern*. San Francisco, Calif.: The Quilt Digest Press, 1991.

Smith, Lois. *Fun & Fancy Machine Quiltmaking*. Paducah, Ky.: American Quilters Society, 1989.

Tyrell, Judi. *Beginner's Guide to Machine Quilting*. San Marcos, Calif.: ASN Publishing, 1990.

Wagner, Debra. *Teach Yourself Machine Piecing & Quilting*. Radnor, Pa.: Chilton Book Co., 1992.

Wolfrom, Joen. *Landscapes & Illusions*. Lafayette, Calif.: C&T Publishing, 1990.

Continuous Patterns

Thompson, Shirley. *Designs for Continuous Line Quilting*. Edmonds, Wash.: Powell Publications, 1993.

"Collection One," "Dimensions Collection," "Romance Collection," "Borders & Corners," "Bouquet Collection," "Celebration Collection," "Miniature Collection," "Renaissance Collection," Hari Walner, Beautiful Publications, 1990–1993. 13340 Harrison St., Thornton, Colo., 80241

About the Author

Maurine Leander Noble became enamored with sewing machines while watching her mother make clothing and draperies for others. She learned a valuable skill at a young age—how to rip out machine stitching! With a degree in home economics education from Oregon State University, Maurine spent many years teaching adult dressmaking, tailoring, machine embroidery, and appliqué classes. Now she teaches machine quilting and related sewing-machine skills exclusively in quilt shops in the Puget Sound area. This book was developed from her classes.